Silent Saturday

Silent Saturday

by

R. Earl Allen

BAKER BOOK HOUSE
Grand Rapids, Michigan

Library of Congress Catalog Card Number: 68-54237

PHOTOLITHOPRINTED BY CUSHING - MALLOY, INC.
ANN ARBOR, MICHIGAN, UNITED STATES OF AMERICA
1 9 6 8

FOREWORD

This volume by Dr. R. Earl Allen, entitled *Silent Saturday,* after one of the tremendously effective sermons in the book, is truly one of the finest volumes I have ever read. The writings of Dr. Allen are always refreshing, and especially and particularly this latest publication concerning the fact and meaning of the glorious ministry and resurrection of our Lord. He is a fortunate preacher who reads the volume and it will be a fortunate congregation who has a pastor who will enrich the preparation of his own message by the spiritual insights of these chapters.

Dr. Allen has published worthy volumes heretofore and I believe that is the reason that he has so studiously sought to make this latest book doubly effective. His studious habits have been reinforced by the earnest desire to add a worthwhile contribution to the sermons he has already published. He has certainly succeeded in this series of messages. His outline for the sermon, "Silent Saturday," is unique. His gifts of alliteration (not strained or mechanical, but dynamic and meaningful) can be seen in every chapter title and, in most instances, throughout the outlines of the sermons themselves. This is but a small part of the rich facets to be found in the book.

May the Lord bless the eyes that look upon these pages and may God bless to all of our hearts and to the needs of the world the triumphant message written on every leaf and seen on every page of this volume. Upon the author and readers alike, may the hope of the incomparable resurrection day come to be the hope of the whole lost world and at the consummation of the age the reality of God's redeemed people.

W. A. CRISWELL
President, Southern
Baptist Convention

PREFACE

The great themes of God's Word hover closely around the passion, resurrection, and return of our blessed Lord. The study of these precious truths is most rewarding. The significance of the sacred, final week of our Lord comes clearly into focus when we realize that nearly one-third of all material in the gospel narratives concerns itself with His passion. Surely, God would want us to know the price of Calvary which revealed God's matchless love. When the cross of Jesus was put into the ground at Golgotha, Christ staked his redemptive claim on all who believe. John 3:16 can never be doubted.

Our debt is to many. We are grateful to the Rosen Heights Baptist Church for prayerfully hearing these messages.

Our deep gratitude goes to friends who read the manuscript and to Dr. W. A. Criswell for writing the Foreword.

I acknowledge my debt to Mrs. Alfred A. Brian, Jr. for sermonic and manuscript help and to Miss Arline Harris for her skillful help in final manuscript preparation.

Grateful acknowledgment is made to my cherished friend, Dr. G. Paul Butler, editor of *Best Sermons* (Volume X), and Trident Press for permission to use my sermon, "Silent Saturday," which was previously published in that volume.

Thank you for reading this far . . . please continue. Gratefully,

R. EARL ALLEN

CONTENTS

1

*Wherefore God also hath highly
exalted him, and given him a name
which is above every name*
(Philippians 2:9).

THE INDESCRIBABLE INDIVIDUAL

"What's in a name?" This question has been immortalized by poets and frequently has engaged the attention of philosophers. The Bible places great emphasis upon names and their meanings. A parenthetical phrase in Numbers 32:38 says "their names were changed." It was possible then, and it is possible now, for a name to be changed. But it is a solemn thing, and it cannot be done without due process of law.

In some cultures, names have been considered very important. They were distinctive, descriptive, and had great personal meaning. Parents often waited until a child showed some progress or had some adventure in life before they gave him a name that signified something of his character or personality.

We live in an impersonal age. Banks once had experienced bookkeepers who gave check signatures careful scrutiny to see if they were authentic before they would certify the checks. Now checks are put into a sorting machine and the numbers printed on them determine distribution into the proper accounts. We have so many numbers applied to us that sometimes men merely seem to be another point of reference in an age that is totally mechanistic.

The name of Jesus Christ will never become just a number. His is the greatest name in human history. It has remained unaltered from before the beginning of time. How can we describe what that Name means to us? We cannot measure it; we cannot number it; our minds cannot encompass the greatness of the Son of God.

This indescribable individual Isaiah attempted to depict some eight hundred years before He appeared: "For unto us a child is born, unto us a son is given, and the government shall be upon his shoulder; and his name shall be called Wonderful, Counselor, The Mighty God, The Everlasting Father, The Prince of Peace" (Isaiah 9:6).

Before a portrait of Christ we may stand with appreciation, seeing through the eyes of the artist the attributes he imagined in that Face. Yet we cannot help feeling that the portrait is imperfect. It does not adequately portray His face — no portrait can. The same is true of His hands — the hands that were nailed to the cross, yet broke bread three days later at a table in Emmaus. It was by His hands that the disciples there recognized Him. Who can describe His hands? What was it like to feel their gentle touch in blessing, in healing, in friendship?

On human lips, the name of Jesus is the sweetest name in any language, Talmadge has said. It is easier, he affirmed, for a child to be taught that name than the word *Mother*. It comes easily to the tongue. It is not a harsh name, but a name of beauty and sweetness.

When Gypsy Smith, an evangelist of a former generation, held a revival meeting in the Will Rogers Coloseum, I was at a very impressionable age. It was the largest religious crowd I had ever seen. Each night the great Gypsy would close his service, after the invitation was finished, singing in his unusually eloquent voice, "Wonderful, wonderful Jesus! In the heart He implanteth a song." He sent us away with that Name singing in our hearts. We could not help but feel that it was a wondrous thing to speak the name of Jesus.

Supreme Name

The New Testament begins with the words, "The book of the generation [genealogy] of Jesus Christ . . ." (Matthew 1:1). In the Bible we find 256 different words trying to portray the Indescribable One. The many names of Christ seem almost inexhaustible, but none is quite so sweet as "Jesus."

The great hymn-writer, Charles Wesley, wrote about the name of Jesus in the hymn, "O For a Thousand Tongues to Sing," which has been a favorite for generations. The third verse reads:

> Jesus — the Name that charms our fears,
>   That bids our sorrows cease;
> 'Tis music in the sinners ears,
>   'Tis life, and health, and peace.

When Jesus taught His disciples to pray, He tried to instill in them a sense of reverence for God. They were to pray, "Hallowed be thy Name." We are not to profane the name of God or of His Son, Jesus Christ. We are not to handle the name of Jesus as though it were common or unimportant. Respect for the name of Jesus Christ needs to be reclaimed today, beginning with those who call themselves Christian. God is omnipresent; His Spirit is with us and within us and dwells in believers over the whole earth. Yet the Name of God or the thought of God must not become common or profane, for He is Holy.

There is a great difference between familiarity with God and informality in worship. When we bow our heads in the house of God, when we call on the name of Jesus Christ, there must be that awesome reverence due the Great God of the universe. That respect should extend to His Son and to His Word.

God's Son and His Word have been the particular point of attack of atheists and infidels. When Thomas Payne disembarked from a ship in America about a century and a half ago, he boasted, "When I get through, there will not be five Bibles left in America." He thought that he could spread his "age of reason" philosophy, and people would abandon the Word of God. But the Bible is still a best seller, and the name of Thomas Payne is almost forgotten. Modern young people frequently ask, "Who was he?"

The name of Jesus Christ has never been popular with everyone, it is true. Only one of the ten lepers He healed came back to fall down before Him. But there will always be some who care, some who follow Him, some who are willing to dedicate their whole lives to Him. Through these, His Name and His message continue to have an impact on the whole world.

It is incredible that any man who comprehends in any measure the holiness of God and the love of Jesus Christ should drag the name of Jesus down into the gutter.

"God also hath highly exalted him," the apostle Paul wrote, "and given him a name which is above every name" (Philippians 2:9). The name *Christ* indicates His position as God's Anointed, His claim to Lordship over the earth. *Christ* in Greek is the same word as *Messiah* in Hebrew. For centuries the Jews had been looking for their Messiah, eagerly awaiting the time God's Deliverer would come to save them from their enemies and rule them in righteousness and peace.

Sacrificial Name

The name *Jesus* (Hebrew: *Joshua*) meant "Saviour." As the angel told Joseph, "Thou shalt call his name *Jesus*: for he shall save his people from their sins" (Matthew 1:21). The name of Jesus Christ stands for the person and work of the Godhead in human affairs. *Jesus* became His name of deep humiliation, His personal name as a man among men, suffering and dying for them.

"Isn't this the son of Mary?" asked some of His contemporaries. "Isn't He the carpenter's son?" Yes, He was the son of Mary, the foster-son of the carpenter, Joseph of Nazareth. The people knew Him only as Jesus — His personal name — not as the Son of God, the Messiah, the Christ.

"I am the good shepherd," He said, "and know my own sheep and they know me. Just as my Father knows me and I know the Father; and I lay down My life for the sheep" (John 10:14-15, *Living Gospels*). He was "the Lamb slain from the foundation of the world" (Revelation 13:8). The accounts of His trial and crucifixion illustrate the prophecies of Isaiah 53.

"No one can kill Me without My consent," He said of Himself. "I lay down My life voluntarily" (John 10:18, *Living Gospels*).

When we come to Calvary, our hearts should overflow with the warm glow of loving gratitude. When we realize that His sacrifice there was substitutionary, that He took our place, we cannot help but love Him.

> See, from His head, His hands, His feet,
> Sorrow and love flow mingled down;
> Did e'er such love and sorrow meet,
> Or thorns compose so rich a crown?
>
> Were the whole realm of nature mine,
> That were a present far too small;
> Love so amazing, so divine,
> Demands my soul, my life, my all.
>
> — Isaac Watts

When the war in Korea first broke out, a woman fleeing from North Korea barely escaped with her life. When she was taken to a hospital, the doctor said, "Your feet will have to be amputated — it is the only way to have your life. Can you do without your feet?" He had no way of knowing this little woman was a Christian.

"I can do without my feet," she answered. "I can do without my hands. I can do without anything in this world, except Jesus!"

Saving Name

The Person and Nature and Name of Jesus Christ cannot be destroyed. We have had mighty men in this world, mighty men of war, mighty men of literature, mighty men of song, but none has had such impact on the world as Jesus Christ. By the spread of His gospel, lives have been transformed. His influence has operated through the centuries and the world is different from what it would have been without Him. Sin and evil permeated the course of mankind from the beginning, but salvation came only through Jesus Christ.

To some people, names are nothing more than a list in the telephone directory. But in the Bible we find that the name of Jesus Christ implies what God is trying to say to us. His Son's name, according to God's purpose, is to have preeminence. One historian has said that at the top of every page of history stands the name of Jesus, because Jesus has walked across history. He has shaped our civilization.

Jesus changed the world's attitude toward childhood. In many non-Christian cultures, some children have been unwanted. Often they were killed or abandoned. But in Christian lands, all children are respected, valued, loved. There are laws in our nation against mistreating them. There are orphanages for those who have no one to care for them.

Jesus also changed the status of womanhood. In His time, they were often considered mere possessions, little more than slaves or animals. The equality and freedom women have in the enlightened parts of the world result from Christian principles applied in society.

He has changed the world's attitude toward the sick and afflicted. Once they were cast off from society, but the Great Physician taught men compassion and set up ideals of healing the sick.

Wordsworth wrote, "Milton, thou shouldst have lived unto this hour!" Such a great man, had he lived on, might have continued to contribute to society, for he had made the world a better place in which to live. But as we call the roll of the mighty men of all ages, we have to say of most of them, "It is better that the world forget such people as Pharoah and Genghis Khan and Hitler."

If you go to a rural cemetery and push back the weeds that overrun the markers, you will find names of those whose voices were powerful in the community in the past, who were able to control the lives and destinies of others while they lived. Now you can walk over their graves as easily as over those of the most helpless. All have been equalized with the passing of time.

But Jesus has no grave over which the sacrilegious may tread with impunity — only an empty tomb into which we gaze with awe. For Jesus lives until this hour. His is the enduring Name. Jesus Christ is still alive.

Pilate, should he be living today, would still be trying to wash his hands, symbolically trying to remove from his soul the guilt, and from his mind and heart the memory of the name of Jesus.

Judas, when he came to that dark garden at midnight, had beguiled himself into thinking that he was kissing the son of Mary, when he was touching the very Face of God.

A French infidel named Voltaire said, "One day I shall crush the wretch Jesus Christ." But when the time came that he was dying, he cried out, "O thou pale Galilean, Thou hast conquered!"

How could Jesus Christ be removed from this world? You would have to take out life, for He is life. You would have to do away with truth, for He is Truth. You would have to forego healing, for He is the Great Physician. You would have to forget teaching, for He is the Great Teacher. You would have to negate power, for He possesses all power. You would have to burn down churches, for He is the Head of the Church. You would have to destroy homes, for He is the heart of the home. You would have to blot out all hope, for He and He alone is the hope of the world.

The gospel of hope began to manifest itself at the cross. Only Jesus Christ could pay the penalty; only He could bear our sin. But the cross without the empty tomb was incomplete. The power of Jesus in our world today is the presence of a living Christ. Isaiah said His name was to be "Emmanuel — God with us." This is more than a Christmas verse — it is a verse for the darkest night. It is a verse for the valley of the shadow of death. It is a verse for the lonely hour, for the desolate heart. It is a verse for the stress of temptation.

"Emmanuel — God with us!" May we apologize to the Spirit of God for our attitude when we live and act as if God were dead. We are so often tempted to think that God cannot do anything with this evil world in which we live. But Jesus Christ is with us, and in Him is all power.

The apostle Paul put a blunt question to those who were not living pure lives: "Know ye not that your body is the temple of the Holy Spirit?" And the Spirit is also "Christ in you, the hope of glory."

How better could we describe His presence with us? He is our only Savior. He is our Confidant, our Counselor. He is our Friend, closer than a brother, who never leaves us nor forsakes us. He knows all about us and yet loves us supremely. He is our Great Physician, the only one who can give balm for our aching hearts, sleep to our weary bodies, rest to our troubled minds, cleansing to our sinful souls. He is, indeed, our Hope of Glory.

What greater name can we call Him than what God named Him: Jesus Christ, Saviour and Deliverer? We may succeed to some extent when we try to put into words what He has meant to us in our experience, although that is difficult. But, bless God, we are able to say of His Name, "It will do when I am dying." This is the Name, the only Name, that you can whisper at the gate of heaven to find a loving welcome from a Heavenly Father. For Jesus said, "Him that cometh unto me I will in no wise cast out."

2

I have yet many things to say unto you, but ye cannot bear them now (John 16:12).

SILENCES OF THE SAVIOUR

Martin Luther prayed, "Oh, Lord God, punish us, but be not silent toward us." The silence of God, to a Christian, is one of the most difficult things he can experience.

Our age does not seem to believe in silence. We are people in a hurry and we surround ourselves with noise. In many homes, the family seems to feel that the television must be on all day whether anyone is watching or not. If the television isn't blaring, music from the stereo or the radio envelops us. We are so accustomed to noise that silence startles and disturbs us.

It was said of Jesus that "Never man spake like this man" (John 7:46). However, a close examination of the Scriptures reveals that Jesus used silence as a method of communication quite as effectively as speech. He realized that tone of voice could aid understanding, but stern silence at certain moments could also convey great meaning.

In reading the Gospels, we often ask ourselves, "What does He mean by these words?" We might also ask, with profit, "What does He mean by being silent at this point?"

It was the custom for many years to print all the words of Jesus in red in the New Testament. It makes an interesting study to search out those instances when the Lord was silent. Why were the lips of Jesus sealed? Why did God have absolutely nothing to say?

When Jesus faced a situation with silence, His disciples must have focused their attention upon Him more completely. On the evening before His death Christ mentioned to His disciples the coming of the Holy Spirit, the third person of the Trinity. "I have yet many things to say unto you," He told them, "but ye cannot bear them now" (John 16:12). The word *bear* actually means to carry. God has far more to say to us than we are willing to hear, more than we are able to understand, more than we are ready to practice. The messages of God often have to wait upon our capacity. Our education is gradual. His revelation is progressive.

"It is expedient for you that I go away," Jesus told His disciples.

"Good Master, what shall we do?" they interrupted, panic-stricken. His silence on some subjects presented a dilemma to them. They were frightened at the prospect of His absence. What could they do? He had been there to say the right words at the proper time for the exact occasion. They depended on Him.

"I will not leave you comfortless," He reassured them. The fact that He had provided another Comforter for them in the future had not occurred to them.

The silences of the Master cannot be ignored. There are several of them, and they can be found in at least three areas. First, there is the majestic silence of the Master as He faced death.

Death

Seven hundred years before Jesus was born of the virgin Mary, Isaiah graphically pictured the Lamb of God who was without spot or blemish. "He was oppressed, and he was afflicted, yet he opened not his mouth . . ." (53:7). The Messiah to come, said Isaiah, would be as a sheep dumb before His shearers. A pig will squeal to the last drop of blood, but the sheep faces death without a bleat. Jesus faced death without a word of protest. The angry Jewish leaders laid hold of Him in the Garden of Gethsemane. They beat Him, spit on Him, mocked Him. Never in history has justice miscarried so completely. But the suffering Saviour opened not His mouth.

Majestically, Jesus stood silently before His accusers and the Roman officials. Why did He not speak?

There are three reasons for His silence. First, He did not speak because He had absolutely nothing to change. If we knew that our life would end at a particular time, there would probably be some preparations we would like to make. We would search the corners of our hearts to make sure that they were clean before God. We would want to change some things. But the Lord had nothing to change. He had lived a perfect life, making no mistakes. He had not uttered one word that He needed to recall. He had left nothing undone. He had completed the task God had sent Him to do. He had the approval of God and man. God had said, "This is my beloved Son in whom I am well pleased." Pilate said, "I find no fault in Him." Jesus was able to face death calmly because He had nothing to change.

Jesus faced death with composure because He had nothing to prove. He did not appear before the tribunal of man to prove He was God. The Judge of all the earth did not have to answer to human judges. Such men had not listened to His message nor followed His teachings. Why then should He reveal to them that He was God, the Creator of the heavens and the earth? Jesus spoke not because death held no terror for Him. On the cross, He deliberately surrendered His spirit back to His Father in heaven.

The Scriptures tell of His burial. His body was put into a grave, and when God was ready, the spirit of Jesus came back to the tomb to lift up the body resting there. The face napkin was folded carefully and laid aside. Jesus was in no hurry. Death had no more power; He was victorious over it. For Him, death was only a step from the cruel cross into the presence of God. After He conquered death, it should hold no lasting terror for any man.

Demand

Jesus also remained silent when He was brought before His doubters. "Don't you understand that I have the power of life and death over you?" Pilate asked. The Roman governor did not realize that he was actually the one on trial, that Jesus held the power of life and death over all the world. Pilate kept insisting that Jesus should defend Himself. Pilate panicked while Jesus stayed perfectly calm. With dignity, He stood silent before those who doubted Him and those who accused Him.

Why did He not defend Himself? Because He was obedient unto death. Nothing that Jesus might have said at that moment — unless He wielded His power as the mighty Son of God — could have stopped the miscarriage of justice. Throughout the night the high priest and his followers pursued their plot, determined that Jesus must die. Nothing could have changed their hearts or their minds.

But there was a better reason why He didn't speak. He remained silent because it was in God's plan. The Bible said He would be obedient unto death, even the death of the cross.

Pilate was anxious to be rid of Jesus. When he discovered that Jesus was a Galilean, he quickly dispatched Him to Herod, who had jurisdiction over Galilee. Herod was the only man to whom Jesus never spoke a single word. With sinners, He was always compassionate. To the despised and rejected, He was ever a friend. Those who called on Him for help, Jesus answered. But when He stood before Herod, He did not dignify that brutal ruler by speaking a word to him. Jesus did not recognize Herod as a king, or even as a man. He stood implacably, sternly silent.

Herod was a lustful man who enjoyed all the entertainment tricks of the world. When he heard that Jesus, who had done many miracles, was being sent to him by Pilate, Herod was pleased. He hoped Jesus would show him His tricks. Herod did not want to meet the great God of the universe. Herod did not want to encounter another convicting prophet like John the Baptist. He wanted only a sideshow Saviour, a carnival Christ. "Let Him come and perform a miracle. Let Him entertain me. Doesn't He know who I am?"

Oh, yes, Herod, He knows who you are! He knows very well that John the Baptist stood before you and challenged every evil, dirty thing that you were doing. He knows you didn't appreciate the whiplash of John's tongue, that eventually you beheaded John the Baptist. John's accusations were no greater horror to Herod, however, than the sting of silence when Jesus looked at him. Jesus looked completely through him, for there was really nothing in him. He was only an evil shadow, a beastly shell. God is not our errand boy who jumps when we crack the whip. When the evil Herod commanded Him to speak, Jesus made no reply.

To the merely curious, the moral coward and the mocking cynic, Heaven always remains silent. If we go to church in the spirit of seeking entertainment, God will not speak to us. We will go away without knowing His presence. Many who have the spirit of Herod come to church saying, in effect, "Sing a tune, do a trick, attract my attention!" Those who seek Heaven as a sideshow will find the Lord strangely quiet. Jesus has no word for ears that will not listen.

Depth

There was depth in the silence of Jesus. There is "a time to keep silence, and a time to speak," said Solomon, the wise old Preacher (Ecclesiastes 3:7). Jesus said, concerning Himself, "Behold, a greater than Solomon is here." There are times when silence is golden and there are times when silence is sin. A sense of timing often makes the difference.

What do we learn from the depths of Christ's silences? He spoke nothing shameful. No gossip passed His lips. Those who wanted to discredit Him came one day, bringing a woman taken in adultery. "Is it right to kill her?" they demanded. The Lord didn't dignify the situation with words. He just began to write in the sand. When He had finished writing, the cowards and hypocrites had slunk away in guilt and shame. He wrote that day because he did not want to publicize the shame of an individual. Jesus never stirred up scandal, He forgave it. He knew the innermost secret of every heart, but no betrayal passed His lips. He taught us that silence is better than accusation.

Jesus showed us that we are not to speak scornfully or sarcastically. When a man loses his temper, he loses far more. Respect and friendships are often lost as well, and many times they cannot be regained. Jesus never spoke scornfully to any man, although He made outright accusations against hypocrisy.

Jesus did not express His sympathy in a multitude of trite words that fall lightly on broken hearts. He wept with His friends in their sorrow.

A woman came to Him one day. "Lord," she said, "I have a child who is possessed of an evil spirit. Oh, Son of David, heal my child!" According to the Scriptures, Jesus said nothing. She was very insistent, and she was a foreigner. The disciples wanted to send her away.

Sometimes, what we want is not what we really need. She came to ask healing for her daughter. She stayed long enough to receive something for herself. If God always gave us the first thing we desired, our lives would be full of secondary things rather than eternal investments. In faith the woman had made a long journey to see the Master. There was the pallor of dust on her face and Jesus could see the love in her heart.

"God, help me," she murmured in humility. When she expressed the need in her own heart to know God, Jesus answered her. "Great is thy faith," He said. For this mother to want her child to be healed was a natural thing, but for her to realize that her own heart needed to be cleansed was more important in the Lord's sight.

The symphony of the soul is a symphony of silence, because things in the depths are unutterable. Love is more often whispered than shouted. One Old World city is built above underground rivers. By day, with the noise of the traffic and the shouts of the people, you can hear nothing. But if you go out late at night and kneel on the sidewalk and put an ear to the pavement, you can hear the flow of the underground springs. "He that hath ears to hear, let him hear" (Matthew 11:15). There are silences that God wants us to hear.

Sunrise and sunset do not speak in tones of thunder, but surely they have messages for our hearts. God said for us to be silent, to be still, to shut out everything else, and know that He is God. Put your ear to the doors of everlasting life and let God speak through silence.

There are some silences of the soul that should be respected and protected. Paul tells of one who "heard unspeakable words, which it is not lawful for a man to utter" (II Corinthians 12:4). In the sanctuary of his own spirit, every man has within him the symphony of his own soul. Revelations have come to him from God that are not always to be shared with others. Perhaps God has spoken to you something which, if you tried to put it into words, would somehow cheapen it, or make it seem foolish. Still, God was very real to you. There are some silent, unutterable things that God has to tell us.

The silences of Jesus should show us when to speak and when to be silent, when to be still and when to act, when to witness and when not to witness. When should we speak? When there is a word to be said for the Lord and His church. When should we never remain silent? When some erring heart wants to find its way back to God. At such times, silence is sin.

It has been said that "Silence is golden." That is true. But never let it become yellow when you should be speaking out for the Lord Jesus Christ.

3

Jesus taketh with him Peter, and
James, and John, and leadeth them
up into an high mountain apart by
themselves: and he was transfigured
before them

(Mark 9:2).

TRIUMPH OF THE TRANSFIGURATION

The most mysterious miracle in all the life of Christ was His transfiguration. If we were listing the main points of His life, we would certainly include His birth, His baptism, His temptation, His crucifixion, and His resurrection. But one of the strangest events was His transfiguration. Often it is passed over lightly because so little is recorded concerning it.

It was a mountaintop experience, but we are not told exactly which mountain. The most likely place seems to be Mount Hermon. It was some distance from Jerusalem. The timing of this event is very important; the greater part of His ministry was finished and the cross loomed in the near future. Little by little the large, curious crowds had dwindled away until only a few faithful followers were left. Peter's great confession had been made, and here we behold the Christ, the Son of the living God, in His glory.

Jesus had taken His disciples to a solitary place for rest and prayer. Then from the twelve, He took the "inner circle" of three with Him to the top of a mountain: Peter, James, and John — the trinity of the New Testament, as Abraham, Isaac and Jacob were the trinity of the Old Testament. Here we are allowed, through the report of the disciples, a reverent glimpse of a sacred moment.

Why should this momentous event in the life of Jesus, this thrilling experience in the life of His disciples, suffer neglect? Perhaps it is because we have no language in which to speak of it. We describe things by association with previous experience. There is no human experience with which we can associate the transfiguration. We understand something of dying, and thus of the crucifixion. We know something of the agony of decision and therefore have some faint idea of His suffering in Gethsemane. But a transfiguration we cannot understand — it is an experience beyond our comprehension.

As Jesus and the disciples toiled physically up the mountainside, our minds must put forth effort to climb the steep ascent up this high hill of the Lord.

This unforgettable moment happened "at the end of the sixth day" — probably in the evening of the beginning of the Sabbath. Surely the grace of God is marvelously manifested to those who wait on the Lord in the day He has set aside. On the Isle of Patmos, the apostle John wrote of an experience many years later when he was given another marvelous vision of the Risen Lord, when he "was in the Spirit on the Lord's day, and heard behind me a great voice, as of a trumpet" (Revelation 1: 10).

The transfiguration was evidently a night scene. We are familiar with spotlights which illumine a performer on stage, but this is lighting from outside the person. The illumination was unusual because it came from within Jesus: "And his raiment became shining, exceedingly white as snow," Mark tells us (9: 3). The change in His face and clothing must have been an unforgettable sight. And again, it is something so far from our experience that we cannot really imagine it.

Perhaps these three disciples had less trouble later, picturing in their minds a glorified Jesus at the Father's right hand. On the mountain they beheld Him conversing with two other shining figures whom they somehow recognized as Moses and Elijah. It was truly a momentous, mysterious, majestic moment.

Proposal

When the startled disciples awakened from heavy sleep and beheld this incredible scene, they were speechless. Who would have known the right thing to say at such a moment? Who would know how to acknowledge the presence of men who had been gone from the earth for hundreds of years?

Perhaps it would have been better if the awed disciples had kept silent, if they had reverently worshiped the Lord in His newly-revealed glory. But Simon Peter — as usual — blurted out the first thing that came to his mind.

"Master," Peter stammered, "it is good for us to be here: let us make three tabernacles; one for thee, and one for Moses, and one for Elias" (Mark 9:5). In other words, his first thought was to hold on to the moment of glory, to cling to it, to preserve the experience indefinitely. "Why don't we stay right here!"

"He knew not what to say," the Bible tells us, "for they were sore afraid" (Mark 9:6).

Have you ever had such a tremendous spiritual experience in your life that you hated for it to end? You might never know that particular joy again; you might never know such an ecstatic moment or feel the presence of God in such power. It would never be quite the same again, and Simon Peter wanted to capture and preserve what he felt at that moment. Peter was greatly exhilarated and wanted to remain there on the mountain top. But his request was foolish. The earth is never prepared to entertain heaven, and those who have been to heaven are never at home on earth any more!

What about the needy people in the valley below? He didn't think of them. We, like Peter, are moved far more by our emotions than by the deep needs of a lost world. It would be so much easier, so much more pleasant to stay on the mountain peak, so much closer to heaven. It is difficult to return to the routine duties of the valley, to the sorrowing world of disillusionment, heartbreak, and sin.

'Is there any need to go back there?" Peter was saying. "Let's stay here!" On the mountain peak we feel very near to God; in the valley we feel the desperate need of God's nearness.

Jesus didn't permit His disciples to build their tabernacles. But about a hundred years ago, a religious group built three buildings on that mountain which they called "churches" for meditation and contemplation. These are little more than museums. The church is not a building; it is a living body of baptized believers banded together in the fellowship of union with Jesus Christ.

Perhaps the disciples were interested in conversing with Moses and Elijah because they understood them better than they did Jesus at that moment. Moses was an old man who was used to mountaintop experiences. God had called him to the top of awesome Mount Sinai and given him the commandments for God's people. Then God had, at the end of Moses' journey, shown him the Promised Land from the top of Mount Nebo. There God buried Moses — no man knows where, we are told.

Elijah had stood on Mount Carmel confronting the powerful priests of Baal. "Hear me, O Lord, hear me," he prayed, "that this people may know that thou art the Lord God" (I Kings 18: 37). In answer, the heavens opened and fire fell. "If the Lord be God," Elijah entreated the people, "follow him!" When God was ready, He sent a chariot of fire to take Elijah to heaven.

It was not possible, however, for the disciples to commune with these two great men of God. After Peter's outburst, Moses and Elijah vanished. Only Jesus remained. There cannot be too much emphasis put on that: *Jesus only!* Neither Moses nor Elijah could be compared with Jesus.

Some recognize Jesus as a master-teacher — but He is not only that. Some say that He was a great and good man, pursuing His cause even to a martyr's death. But He was more than a man;

He *is* the Son of God. He is the "great unlike." There is no one who can be compared with Him as the whole book of Hebrews proclaims. Jesus only! If we know and have fellowship with great servants of God, that is fine. But the most important thing is to know Jesus and worship Him — Jesus only!

Purpose

What was the purpose of this unique miracle? First, it was to strengthen Jesus for the ordeal before Him, "a taste of rest to the weary traveler," as Professor David Smith put it. The disciples overheard part of the conversation. They were talking about the decease of Jesus at Jerusalem.

Jesus was as much God as if He were never man, and as much man as if He were never God. In His humanity, He had come to a great moment of choice. He could have ascended from this mount of heavenly glory straight home to rejoin His Father — or He could descend the mountain and go forward to the cross. He chose to go on to His death in Jerusalem, to fulfill His role as the Lamb of God.

This experience strengthened Jesus for the difficult days ahead, for the kiss of Judas, the denials of Peter, the antagonism of the crowd, the nakedness of the cross. We hear in the background the faint prelude of Gethsemane: "Father, if there be any other way. . . ."

Moses had been put to sleep by God, and Elijah had been translated into heaven, but Jesus was transfigured before men. There is a vast difference. Moses represented the Law; he was Israel's great lawgiver, the one who received the commandments from the hand of God. Elijah represented the prophets; he was a reformer, a spokesman for God to His erring people, a crusader for righteousness. He demanded that Israel remember the laws of God and obey them. Jesus was the link, for He said, "Think not that I am come to destroy the law, or the prophets: I am not come to destroy, but to fulfill" (Matthew 5:17).

The transfiguration was intended not only to strengthen Jesus for His sacrifice, but to strengthen the disciples. In a little while they would be scattered and disillusioned. Christ was preparing them for trying days. We also need to draw from the glorified Christ strength to face the difficult experiences of life — every frustrating day, every painful experience, every shadow of despair.

Peter, James and John had never known Moses and Elijah, but they recognized them. There was no formal presentation; it must have been a divine revelation. The body of Moses had been buried up in the mountain, and Elijah had been translated, yet they had continuity of life in recognizable bodies.

These three disciples could never be the same again. No man is ever the same after he sees Christ high and lifted up, as Isaiah saw God in the experience he recorded in the sixth chapter of his prophetic book. The disciples described Jesus' clothes as "white as snow, so as no fuller on earth can white them" (Mark 9:3). They saw Him for the first time in His celestial body. His transfiguration began from the inside and literally glowed out until the very body itself seemed transformed. They recognized something of the glory of eternity in that moment. These men, more than any others, must have gained an idea of what heaven will be like.

Pattern

When we glimpse the glory of the Risen Christ, we want to be like Him. But we realize far too seldom that something of the glory of eternity surrounds the Christian all the time — although we can't see it.

In the Old Testament, we are told how the nameless servant of Elisha thought they were done for. In dismay he said, "Alas, my master! What shall we do?"

"Fear not," Elisha reassured him, "for they that are with us are more than they that are with them." Then Elisha prayed, "Lord, open his eyes, that he may see."

The Bible says the young man then saw that "the mountain was full of horses and chariots of fire round about Elisha" (II Kings 6:17).

In one sense, the transfiguration experience was possible only to Jesus. Yet His transfiguration gives us a preview of our celestial bodies. Concerning this life also, however, God has a word to say to His discouraged children: "Be *ye* transformed!" We are to be transfigured in life before men so that they may see God in us.

What is the transformation Christ works in a man's life and how does it happen? God does not whitewash just the outer life. Jesus called the men who attempted self-cleansing and boasted in their self-righteousness, "whited sepulchers." Rather, God cleanses and renews the soul of man. When this change takes place in the inner man, his countenance, his walk, and his talk will not be the same. "Be ye transformed," the apostle Paul wrote, "by the renewing of your mind, that ye may prove what is that good, and acceptable, and perfect, will of God" (Romans 12:2).

When Moses came down from Mount Sinai after talking with God, the Bible tells us, "Moses knew not that the skin of his face shone" (Exodus 34:29). He didn't know it, but the people saw it. If you have been with Jesus, people will be conscious of the difference that He has made in you. "Let your light so shine before men," He said, "that they may see your good works, and glorify your Father which is in heaven" (Matthew 5:16).

When Stephen, the first Christian martyr, was being stoned to death outside the gates of Jerusalem, he prayed in the same spirit as Jesus had prayed on the cross, "Lord, lay not this sin to their charge" (Acts 7:60). And the Bible says, "All that sat in the council, looking steadfastly on him, saw his face as it had been the face of an angel" (Acts 6:15). Why? Because he saw and spoke to God.

There can be no transformation of life until there has been a transformation of the prayer life. Jesus went up to the mountain to pray and was transfigured. When Moses talked with God, when Stephen prayed, seeing the Risen Christ standing to welcome him to heaven, it shone in their faces. When we pray, transformation will be revealed in us.

There is no other way to capture that inward radiance which was so evident to those who looked into the face of Jesus. That is why artists say that the most difficult of all portraits to attempt is the face of Christ. Also, we have no way of knowing how He really looked.

Transformation of spirit will produce transformation of life. The apostle Paul said: "But we all, with open face beholding . . . the glory of the Lord, are changed into the same image from glory to glory, even as by the Spirit of the Lord" (II Corinthians 3:18).

There can be a transformation in us if we are willing to present ourselves to God without reservation and let the Spirit perform His sanctifying work in us. We shall be changed from the image of the earthly to the image of the heavenly. In this day when the world seeks a God they do not know, may we show forth His glory that He may be found in us!

4

And being in an agony he prayed
more earnestly; and his sweat was,
as it were, great drops of blood
falling down to the ground

(Luke 22:44).

SUFFERINGS OF THE SAVIOUR

There are two gardens in the Bible that are important in our
soul's salvation. One is the Garden of Eden — *Paradise Lost* is
represented there. The other is the Garden of Gethsemane.
These two gardens were arenas of destiny — not the place of
the world's championship, but the place of the world's salvation.
The world's greatest silent battle was fought in Gethsemane.
All the forces of evil, all the powers of darkness, and all the
fiends of the flesh — all of these converged against Christ there.

The garden called Gethsemane had been known only as a
little grove on the slopes of the Mount of Olives, across the
valley east of Jerusalem. It was a geographic location, but it
has become a synonym for the deepest experience of sorrow
man can know.

After Jesus observed the Passover supper with His disciples,
He had many things to say to them. The hours wore on. Late
at night, those who remained went with Him across the valley
to rest in the tranquil spot called the Garden of Gethsemane.

It is somewhat on the side of the hill, and today it is a

tourist attraction. Every day of the year people are milling around, poking against the trees, hoping the guard or the guide will turn away so that they can snatch a souvenir. When they come back, they say, "Yes, I've been to Gethsemane."

I have been there — and yet I haven't. Geographically we can visit the place, but I doubt if any of us have shared anything of the sorrow, suffering, and agony that Jesus experienced that night. I doubt if we can say that we have actually been to Gethsemane with Him.

"I come to the Garden alone," we sing, "while the dew is still on the roses." But do we mean that? Throughout the dark hours of Jesus' anguish, do not our eyes grow heavy with sleep like those who were supposed to watch outside the gate? Eight were there and three were inside with the Master, about the distance of "a stone's cast."

As we approach Gethsemane, we should heed the admonition God gave Moses at the burning bush: "Put off thy shoes from off thy feet, for the place whereon thou standest is holy ground" (Exodus 3:5). In Gethsemane, we enter into the Holy of Holies in the life of Jesus.

Few have been the times God has pulled back the curtain to reveal the depths of His soul as here. In Old Testament times, when the priest went into the tabernacle, in the outer court he first offered sacrifice for the sins of the people. Then he went beyond the veil, into the Holy of Holies, and there presented the blood of the sacrifice at the Mercy Seat. Anyone other than the High Priest entering that awesome place would be struck dead. Only after the crucifixion of Christ was the veil of the Temple torn open so that everyone was able to peer into this hallowed room which was considered the abode of God on earth.

In the Gospels, the disciples — especially John — described what took place in Gethsemane. "How could they?" you may ask, "Weren't they asleep?"

They slept fitfully, perhaps. They could not have been completely unmindful of the sorrow of Jesus. They were supposed to be His friends; surely they knew something of His heaviness of heart. Or perhaps there came a time during His resurrection ministry when Jesus sat down and told them what had happened that night in Gethsemane. He may have opened to them His heart just as He did that day on the Emmaus Road when He walked with two disciples and opened to them the Scriptures concerning Himself.

Imagine how His "inner circle" must have felt when they heard Him say, "Sleep on now, and take your rest! The time has passed. I don't need you as much as I did."

Their greatest mistake was in thinking that this night was for sleeping. They did not have spiritual perception. They did not have the insight to recognize His sorrow. So they slept, thinking this night would be much like all other nights.

Solitude

When the Lord told His disciples what happened in Gethsemane, first of all He told them about the solitude of His soul. This was the exceeding heaviness of the Man of Sorrows. It was a strange solitariness, an unusual loneliness. There are various solitudes, some by space and others by spirit. Jesus and His disciples were about twenty paces apart, and yet eternity separated them. This Garden witnessed the greatest anguish of the Master — if possible, even more than the cross. For it was here that the battle of the cross was won.

The sun sees enough of the sorrows and tragedies of the world, but the moon sees more than the sun. For there is more sin and sorrow, more violence and wickedness in the darkness. The evil of this world flourishes under the cover of night. The moon looked down on that night on the holiest and sorest sorrow that ever came into any man's life.

Paul's beloved physician-friend, Luke, wrote a vivid description, though he was not there: "and being in an agony. . . ." These words fit most of life's stories! Every man comes to some night of nights and knows something of being in agony.

For Jesus it wasn't the burden of one lost sheep, or one straying boy, or one erring father, or one backslidden loved one — it was the combined sorrows of the entire world that weighed Jesus down with loneliness and agony.

Because of His intense suffering for us, our suffering becomes more bearable. Every man finds here a kinship with Jesus. Yonder in the wilderness when He was tempted, and here in the Garden, we find a feeling of fellowship with Jesus that we never find any other place, for we know a little about sorrow and agony.

On the part of those He loved and defended, there seemed to be little concern. There was, instead, insensitiveness, cowardice, and lethargy. Judas kissed Him. Simon Peter cursed Him. Thomas doubted Him. The Phillips translation of Matthew 26:38 reads, "My heart is in bitter anguish, . . . stay here and keep watch with me."

They failed Him, and they could easily have tried to alibi themselves with the excuse, "Lord, all we are doing is sleeping!" But is there anything worse than sleeping when God needs us? Is there anything worse than indifference in time of revival? Is there anything worse than not standing up to be counted in a moral crisis? We can never fully enter into the sorrow of the Lord's moment of despair in Gethsemane and the suffering He endured — but we should try!

"My God, my God, why hast thou forsaken me?" Jesus cried out from the cross. We look back on the cross that saves, but a cross also shatters. We will have both experiences in our lives. The cross that came into the life of Abraham shattered him — could he slay his son of promise at God's command? The cross that came into the life of Job shattered him — his wife advised, "Curse God and die!"

The cross that came into the life of Christ shattered Him — the holy, sinless one became sin for us. "If he be the King of Israel," sneered the religious leaders of God's people, "let him come down now from the cross, and we will believe him"

(Matthew 27:42). "If thou be the Christ," railed one of the desperate, dying thieves, "save thyself and us!" (Luke 23:39). The cross saved us, but for our sake, Jesus could not save Himself.

Subjection

There would be no remedy for the agony we all suffer through sin in this life or in the life to come if in the Garden Jesus had not said, "Father, thy will, not mine, be done!" He was offered a cup of bitterness which became our cup of blessing. We say that God answers prayer. Did His Son's prayer go unnoticed by Him? It seems that way to some people.

Jesus looked at the cup and recoiled from it, the Bible tells us. This was a natural reaction of the flesh. This earthly tabernacle in which we live is not self — soul is self. You may wear a new suit that makes you recoil from something that might soil it. There is an instinctive recoil of the body from things that might injure it. Jesus came down from heaven and wore the flesh of man for a reason and a season!

What was in this cup? Jesus, the sinless One, looked in it and saw the horror of the cross to His holy nature. He is the only One who has ever been able to say, "Behold, and see if there be any sorrow like unto my sorrow" (Lamentations 1:12). We may have said it, but we can't mean it in the measure to which Jesus meant it.

"Father, if it be possible, let it pass from me!" He cried out. Why? What was in the cup? The distilled accumulation of Adamic sin. Everything, past, present, and future — my sins, your sins, all of them put together, poured into that cup. All the sin of mankind inside the cup. All our poisonous hate and vindictiveness. All the pain that suffering, loneliness, and sorrow can bring was distilled in the cup. Jesus became sin for us, and when He did, God could no longer look upon His Son, because He could not look upon sin. Jesus became sin in our place.

The agony of His suffering was almost unbearable, perhaps the more because it was spiritual and not physical, like the pain of the cross itself. His disciples were already beginning to account Him and His cause a failure. One of them had sold Him out, and the others would desert or deny Him. Didn't God care any more? Didn't God care for His Son? There hasn't been a cry of sorrow on earth as deep, as all-inclusive as the one Jesus made in Gethsemane.

His cup of sorrow ultimately became our cup of salvation. His agony was climaxed with the glorious submission of the Son to the will of His Father. "If there be any other way," He prayed. At first there was revulsion, but the Son was willing: "If not, Thy will be done!"

Whoever counts on any other way of salvation except the cross is lost, doomed, damned. There is no other way! If God let Jesus go to the cross when there was another way, He would have been guilty of great cruelty. God allowed His own Son to be nailed to the cross because there was no other way to save us. The way of morality, the way of human goodness, the way of material offerings — these will not suffice.

"I am the way, the truth, and the life," Jesus said. "No man cometh unto the Father, but by me" (John 14:6). What we call the Lord's prayer — "Our Father, which art in heaven" — is the pattern for prayer that Jesus gave His disciples. Here is the Lord's own, His deepest prayer: "Nevertheless, not my will, but thine be done!"

In Eden, Adam and Eve said in effect, "Not thy will be done, God, but mine!" In Gethsemane we find the Son saying the reverse: "Not my will be done, but thine." This is our Lord's prayer; this is the prayer we need to say on our faces before God: "Not my will, but *thine!*"

Jesus was fully conscious of what His prayer meant: the bitter cup of the cross. We must confess that we know nothing about His purity or holiness; we do not know about sorrow or about praying as He did. We may say, "Lord, we want cleansing, whatever the cost." Sometimes we don't know the price of what we are asking.

But when Jesus said, "Father, thy will be done," He knew what it would cost Him. In the crucible of Gethsemane, His love and the Father's love were welded together to forge our salvation.

5

But we see Jesus, who was made
a little lower than the angels . . .
that he by the grace of God should
taste death for every man

(Hebrews 2:9).

CENTRALITY OF THE CROSS

If we were not so familiar with the story of the cross, if we could hear it anew as if for the first time, perhaps we could regain a sense of the awe and mystery of God's love. The old rugged cross should be, not something in the back of our minds, but in the front of our hearts.

Unfortunately, the contrary is often true. When we get to the story of Calvary we have a mental block. The glory of the transfiguration lifts our hearts. The miracle of Jesus making five loaves of bread and two little fishes feed five thousand people — this captures our imagination. He was able to make the blind see and the lame walk and the dead breathe again. These healings make us rejoice. But when we come to His crucifixion, we shake our heads.

How can we face the reality of the cross? It is death, and it is ugly. The Roman Empire, which used the cross as the chief form of capital punishment, admitted it was vile and brutal. No Roman citizen, regardless of his crime, had to suffer the death of the cross. The cross was reserved for slaves and foreigners.

It seems strange that He who made heaven and earth was considered a foreigner when it came to dying. Truly, He had no home. "The birds of the air have nests," He said, "but the Son of man hath not where to lay his head" (Matthew 8:20). He had no place to be born, only an unused manger. He had no place to die — only a criminal's cross. His own people said, "He is an alien. He is not one of us. Crucify him!"

The God-man who made the earth died as a foreigner. France had its guillotines, England its chopping blocks, but Rome the barbaric cross. Crucifixion was cruel and callous and always done in public. It served as a reminder, insuring good behavior to those who saw it, for a long time afterward.

We do not even like to talk about Gethsemane. It is not only a locality; it is an adjective implying agony, and we shrink from it. But we must face the cross, for it is the focal point of the gospel.

Charles Spurgeon, one of the greatest preachers who ever lived, was accused of the fact that his sermons were all just alike.

"You are right," Spurgeon answered. "I take a text and make a beeline for the cross every time I preach." Unless we magnify the atoning death of Jesus on the cross, we are not preaching the gospel of Christ, regardless of whatever else we might say.

Christ was not the first man to be crucified, nor was He the first man to die for the cause of righteousness. But He was the first and only man ever *to die in our place*. At Golgotha, God was at His best, and man was at his worst! Some of the things they did to Jesus freeze us! But the physical agony He sustained was not His only suffering. It is difficult to talk about, but the shame of the cross is one of the most humiliating things that Jesus endured.

Most of the religions of the world are religions for men — women have no place. The only religion that has a central place for women is Christianity. Men were scarce when Jesus died, just like they are scarce today, many times, when we wish they would stand with us. Women stood around His cross, shameful sight though it was. The hardened soldiers stripped from the suspended bodies all clothing. Criminals were shamed and humiliated in their exposure before the world. No wonder these soldiers expected to be cursed. They looked at Jesus in surprise when He had no harsh words for them. The centurion shook his head and said, "Surely this was the Son of God!"

Secular history tells us that soldiers who drew this detail of death used cheap wine made of hissop to steel their nerves, to fortify themselves when they struck the nails and when they saw the blood and heard the cries of those they crucified.

Voluntary Suffering

It seems incredible that on the part of Jesus this was a voluntary suffering. "I lay down my life . . .," He said, "No man taketh it from me" (John 10:17-18). Also, He said, "Greater love hath no man than this, that a man lay down his life for his friends" (John 15:13). I wonder if He thought He had a friend in that group. They were all His enemies there. God did not force Jesus out of heaven, push Him into the world and make Him go to the cross. But from the foundation of the world, from the time of Adamic sin, God said that Eve's seed should bruise the serpent's head, though "thou shalt bruise his heel" (Genesis 3:15).

The whole scheming, scorning, sinful world thought this was the end of Jesus and all His work. Apparently no man was ever so ingloriously defeated, so ignominiously crushed, so completely dead. He was nailed to a tree — helpless, shamed and in terrible pain.

But that is not the whole story. Yonder at the portals of heaven, twelve legions of angels strained to come to His rescue — 172,000 of them waited for His command, but Jesus did not utter the word. Voluntarily He took upon Himself the burden of sin that caused God to turn away because He was too holy to look upon sin.

Jesus told His disciples beforehand that He would be rejected and humiliated. 'For he shall be delivered unto the Gentiles, and shall be mocked, and spitefully entreated, and spitted on: and they shall scourge him, and put him to death: and the third day he shall rise again" (Luke 18:32-33).

The betrayal of Judas Iscariot, the denial of Simon Peter, the ignominious death on the cross — all this was endured by the world's most sensitive man. At His arrest, the disciples concluded that His was a lost cause; now it was every man for himself, and they fled in terror. Only the women remained.

Do you realize that the world spit on the Saviour? People today are shocked when unruly crowds spit at an ambassador. But mocking onlookers spit upon Jesus. Imagine, people spitting in the face of God — and God not striking them dead! How much the Son of God suffered at our hands! They taunted Him, "If thou be the Son of God, come down!"

It wasn't the first time that men of God have been challenged to come down and leave what God told them to do. Nehemiah was rebuilding the walls of Jerusalem when critics and enemies called, "Nehemiah, come down and parley with us."

"I am doing a great work, and I cannot come down," Nehemiah retorted firmly.

"Prove to us that you are the Son of God!" said the skeptics to Jesus. But He didn't need to prove anything. He *was* the Son of God. When you are something, you don't have to prove it. It is when you are not sure of yourself that you have to prove it.

"Come down from the cross," the crowd taunted Him. The great Son of God, Redeemer of heaven and earth, was like Nehemiah: "I am doing a great work and I *cannot* come down."

Thomas Carlyle, a famous English agnostic, hesitated in front of a show window in Paris as he looked at a crucifix. He said — half to himself, but those who were walking with him overheard him — "Little man, you have had your day!" That's what he thought about Jesus. The priests, the scribes, the soldiers, and Pilate thought, "Little man, you have had your day."

Jesus had commanded the winds and waves and multiplied the loaves and fishes, but He had had His day, His enemies thought.

No, He hadn't had His day. He *was* having His day! He was doing what He had come to do. He was making atonement for sin, and He will yet have His day; for there is a great day coming! He shall return in all of His glory as Judge and Ruler of the earth. Then wicked men won't sneer at Him. They will cry to the rocks and the hills to fall on them and hide them from His sight.

Vicarious Suffering

His was a vicarious suffering. The Bible says, "the Son of man came not to be ministered unto, but to minister, and to give his life a ransom for many" (Matthew 20:28). The most blessed event in all history is the atonement of Jesus — not the advent of Jesus, but the atonement of Jesus.

The word *atonement* which we hear so often and which we rarely fully understand, means *to cover*. His was a vicarious death in that He died for our sin, not His own. The basic concept is to reconcile those who have been separated, making possible a reunion. Christ removed the sin that built a barrier between us and God, uniting us with our Father.

What does *vicarious* mean? Webster says, "Vicarious suffering in the place of one as assumed by another." It is acting as or being a substitute for another. It is the doctrine of the scapegoat taught in the Old Testament, where the high priest symbolically put upon the scapegoat the sins of the people and it was sent into the wilderness. The Bible talks about the scapegoat "taking away" sins.

Isaiah does not talk about an animal, but about a man, the God-man: "All we like sheep have gone astray; we have turned every one to his own way, and the Lord hath laid on him [Jesus] the iniquity of us all" (53:6).

When people were praising John the Baptist, he protested: "I indeed baptize you with water unto repentance: but he that cometh after me is mightier than I, . . . he shall baptize you with the Holy Ghost, and with fire" (Matthew 3:11). "Behold the Lamb of God," John declared, pointing Jesus out to his disciples, "that taketh away the sin of the world" (John 1: 29). For "without shedding of blood there is no remission [of sin]" (Hebrews 9:22).

Jesus was the only one who ever had a life to give away! We can't die for ourselves because we don't own ourselves. We are the slaves of sin. You cannot sell or give away mortgaged property because you don't own it outright; at least part of it belongs to another. We are mortgaged property, if you please. Sin has left its stain on us and we are worthless. The stench of death is already upon us, and we are fit for nothing but the dump heap.

When Christ the Son of God died, it seemed to His followers that all hope was gone. The sun had set and it was dark forever.

Victorious Suffering

But Christ's suffering was victorious! "God hath raised [Him] up, having loosed the pains of death: because it was not possible that he should be holden of it," Luke wrote (Acts 2:24). It wasn't possible that any grave in this whole world could hold Him. His seeming defeat turned into victory. When He cried on the cross, "It is finished!" those words were a victorious shout that has reached down through the ages of this earth to this hour. For Jesus, death ended in victory. When He was crucified, as He suffered scorn and shame and agony, the onlookers said, "He's done for!" But it was not what it seemed.

Sin and evil had done its worst and left its mark, for He will always bear the nailprints in His hands. Even today it has made its inroads on the church. Men try to say the church is worthless and might as well be scrapped. But it is not as weak as it seems. God still lives. God still is on His throne, and He still keeps His promises. God isn't dead and God hasn't had His day. His Great Day is yet to come.

In a past century, when long-distance communication was nothing more than flag signals, a great battle was being fought. Before darkness closed in over the English channel, flags on the shore of France spelled out, "Wellington defeated." All night long the terrible news spread across England. It seemed that the cause of liberty was doomed. But when the morning came, the signalman repeated the message and was able to complete it: "Wellington defeated the enemy!" What rejoicing followed that night of sorrow!

We are awaiting God's daybreak for the completed message. It seems now that night is dark and weeping is constant. But one of these days Jesus Christ is coming back in victory. "Weeping may endure for a night," wrote the Psalmist, "but joy cometh in the morning" (Psalm 30:5).

We must never leave Jesus hanging on the cross, as some do. There was triumph on that Tree; on Golgotha, God won the victory. Our Lord's suffering was voluntary; it was vicarious. But more than anything else, it was victorious! He won the battle and conquered sin for all eternity.

6

*And now when the even was come,
because it was the preparation, that
is, the day before the sabbath,
. . . and when the sabbath was
past . . .*

(Mark 15:45–16:1).

SILENT SATURDAY

In the hearts of all men, whether they recognize it or not, exists a yearning for immortality. This quest is one of the basic drives of a man's life, the search for the eternal. The message of Easter reminds us annually, at least, that life is not hopeless, that death is not the end. If we grasp anew the glorious truth and daring hope that because Jesus Christ died and rose again, we also may overcome death, that dread last enemy, it puts a song in our hearts. His resurrection marked the day that changed the world.

There seems to be a strong element of respectability about attending church on Easter. Everyone likes to feel that he is a part of that which is good and noble. Perhaps there is a larger reason, a more personal reason, in the hearts of some. They seek renewal of spirit. Day after day they are buffeted by the problems of the world. They have become conscious of the weaknesses and failures. They recognize a desperate need of forgiveness for the blight of sin in their lives. With a sense of re-

dedication many come to the house of God on Easter —
as they might also come on any day when need presses them,
seeking renewal of faith and strength.

Whether we seek a living faith, or a renewing of our faith,
we must turn our eyes to a risen Saviour, not a dead example.
We sing joyfully, "Christ Arose!" The true purpose of attending
Easter services is to reassert the reality of the resurrection in our
own lives, not just to observe a tradition. In our human experience, death cancels out life. But we are reminded that
life can cancel out death because Christ overcame death with
life.

A warden of San Quentin, in his memoirs, told of one prisoner
on death row who sent for him in the middle of the night before
his execution. Earlier, the condemned man had brushed off the
efforts of the chaplain to talk with him, but as the time drew
near, the prisoner called for the warden and asked him anx-
iously, "Sir, what's going to happen to me?"

"The government will take care of everything," the warden
assured him. "Don't worry about that."

"That's not what I mean," the condemned man protested.
"You're talking about my body. I'm talking about *me* — what's
going to happen to *me?*"

The idea that we should cease to exist is repulsive to us. "I
believe in the immortality of the soul," Helen Keller declared,
"because I have immortal longings." On Easter we realize anew
that we are important not only to ourselves and to our loved
ones, but to our Creator Himself.

"What do you believe about personal immortality?" was the
question asked Harvard psychiatrist William James by one of
his former students. "I never believed in it very strongly," the
great professor answered, "but I find I believe in it more and
more as I grow older."

That is true of most of us. As we grow older, as we experience the problems of life and the sorrows of losing our loved
ones, we desire more and more to cling to the hope of immortality. The non-religious man as well as the religious man uni-

versally echoes the question of Job, "If a man die, shall he live again?" (14:14).

There are four different concepts about life after death. Those who hold materialistic philosophies think that death is final. There is nothing beyond. We die like animals, and that is all. This view is fatalistic, the view of annihilation.

The philosopher's concept of death is release. Plato and Socrates taught that when we are separated from this body we are released from all the restrictions of life on this earth. That which had been good and beautiful in our lives lingers after our death, influencing those who come after us, but the individual himself has no conscious afterlife. This concept has been expressed with a sarcastic twist: "Life is a bad joke that isn't even funny, and the only way you can get out of it is by dying."

Reincarnation is a widely held oriental concept which says that death changes us from one form into another. We do not cease to exist; we live again in another form: a blade of grass, an animal, another person. This belief cannot satisfy the soul that desires personal immortality.

These three concepts are very different from the Christian doctrine of bodily resurrection. By His death and resurrection, Jesus affirmed that not only does the human spirit survive, but the man himself, consciously and physically, shall survive. Death always leads to resurrection – whether it be for good or ill. The word *resurrection* actually means "to be raised up bodily." The reality of Jesus' resurrection implies the resurrection of physical as well as spiritual life in a celestial, glorified body.

The resurrected body of Jesus was different in some respects from the one He had possessed for thirty-three years. After his resurrection, Jesus could see and hear, walk and eat; He could be touched. At the same time, He possessed the additional ability to appear and disappear, to walk through closed doors, as if space and physical limitations as we know them had no more power over Him. Yet He was recognizable – He had the same physical body that went to the cross and was laid in the grave. His spirit never went into death. He committed His spirit into the hands of God, His Father, in His fourth word from the cross.

"Do you believe," Jesus asked the sisters of Lazarus — "Do you believe that your brother shall live again?"

"Lord, I know that my brother shall be raised again in the last day," Martha responded. But she did not comprehend that resurrection was possible in the here and now, that eternal life exists in the present as well as in the future. That new life which began in Lazarus when He believed in Jesus as the Son of God could not die, but was eternal.

"I am the resurrection, and the life," Jesus assured Martha. "He that believeth in me, though he were dead, yet shall he live: And whosoever liveth and believeth in me shall never die. Believest thou this?" (John 11:25-26)

That is the question we should ask ourselves and each other: "Believest thou this?" The sentence that Jesus spoke just before He asked that question outlines the Christian concept of future life: "Whosoever liveth and believeth in me shall never die."

We never cease to live; only the body dies. The spirit goes home to God who gave it. When the resurrection trumpet calls, the body shall be raised. Then spirit *and* body, reunited, shall be forever with the Lord. This is Christ's complete and final answer to the threat of death and the grave.

Fateful Friday

Go with me in your imagination, if you will, to the city of Jerusalem for the end of what we call "Passion Week." Three unusual days rewrote the history of the world. Three momentous days. In them Jesus of Nazareth, the Son of God, consummated His mission to the world — the days of His death!

The first of these three days is marked on the Christian calendar as "Good Friday." It is difficult to think of the day our Lord was crucified as being "good." Probably a better description is "Black Friday" — the day of the cross, the day of death, the day of darkness.

In American economic history, the term "Black Friday" has been applied to that dismal day during the depression when the stock market failed and many men jumped to their death in despair. Certainly it was the blackest day in our financial history as a nation. In more recent years we have had another national "Black Friday." The tragic assassination of our youngest president gave Friday, November 22, 1963, a memory clothed with sable darkness.

Indeed, what label is sufficient to describe the horror of the day in Jerusalem when God's Son died? Darkness fell at noonday because God closed His eyes and turned His head from the awful scene. God Himself is the light of the world, and when He turned away from that hill called Golgotha, the sun also refused to lend its light. The earth quaked and reeled on its axis. Graves opened of themselves, and the veil of the Temple was ripped from top to bottom. God's creatures were murdering their Maker; mankind was killing God.

How can they call it "Good Friday," that day God died?

That day man's worst evil was turned into God's best blessing. The Crucified One became, not the victim, but the victor. In voluntary humiliation and self-abasement, our Lord Jesus Christ allowed Himself to be put to death by mankind. "And being found in fashion as a man, he humbled himself, and became obedient unto death, even the death of the cross" (Philippians 2:8). On that momentous day man's initial disobedience was offset by Christ's atoning obedience. He became sin for us and suffered — bleeding and dying at the hands of men — the complete penalty for sin, which is separation from God.

Death on the cross was considered so ignominious that no Roman citizen could be executed by that form of punishment no matter how terrible his crime. But He who was the First Citizen of Heaven, He who was God's Son in the flesh, was counted less than a citizen of Rome by mankind whom He had come to redeem. He who owned earth and heaven was treated as an alien slave and put to death on a cross of shame.

It was a fearful Friday, a day of dead hopes, a day of unimaginable sufferings, a day of human beastliness and brutality. "If he be God," a fellow-sufferer sneered, "let him save himself and us." He was spat upon, beaten, ridiculed, harrassed almost to the point of death before a nail touched His flesh.

The mother of Jesus stood in the outer circle around the cross and died a little bit, too. She recalled the words told her in His babyhood: "The sword shall pierce thy heart also." Each of the seven times her Son spoke brought pain to her. Some of His words were shouts of triumph, some were pleas of prayer. Some were half-audible, but all were loving and compassionate.

"Father, forgive them," were His first words, "for they know not what they do." After the darkness passed, soldiers came to break His bones, because in a few hours the great Feast of the Passover must be observed. But they did not find it necessary to hasten His death. He was dead already of a broken heart.

How did David know, a thousand years before, when he wrote, "He keepeth all his bones; not one of them is broken" (Psalm 34:20)? The centurion in charge cried out, "Truly this was the Son of God." The mourning women and the defeated disciples departed.

Joseph of Arimathaea and Nicodemus claimed the body of Jesus and buried it in the new tomb belonging to Joseph. "He made his grave with the wicked," Isaiah had prophesied, "and with the rich in his death" (53:9). How did Isaiah know, except God had revealed it to him? The wealthy young nobleman of the Kingdom of Judah who became God's great messianic prophet understood more clearly than most that the rich, also, have a claim in the sacrifice of God's Son.

Silent Saturday

Following that Fateful Friday came a silent Saturday. Both sacred and secular history are strangely reticent about this particular Sabbath. The Gospel writers skipped over it; Josephus said nothing about it; secular history has ignored it. Saturday was a silent day.

What happened when the world thought God was dead? Was that day blank? What went on during those horrible, numb hours when it seemed that hope had fled?

With sanctified imagination, if you will, please reflect with me on those hours. The day before, crowds had thronged the streets of Jerusalem shouting, "Crucify Him." Today they were tired, and the Passover Sabbath was supposed to be a quiet day, a time when each family group gathered within the house for the sacred observance. It was a feast of holy rejoicing because of the great deliverance God had wrought for the Israelites when He rescued them from Egyptian bondage more than a thousand years before.

Just before the sun went down on Friday, the body of Jesus had been laid in a borrowed tomb. For those closest to Him, life seemed to stand still. But there were, nevertheless, several kinds of emotional response. The women continued to mourn. Surely His mother did not cease her grief. Her sobbing went on through the night. And Mary Magdalene and the others — what did they do? They grieved and planned still to minister to the body of the One who had done so much for them. Was the Passover able to speak to their hearts with hope and faith that the same God could still deliver?

In the Temple, there must have been uneasiness among the priests as they investigated the torn curtain which had bared to their startled eyes the sacred relics of the Most Holy Place. Did they hurriedly bind it together again? They had secured from Pilate permission to station soldiers at the tomb. Did they go themselves to check, to make very, very sure that this disturber-of-the-peace was silenced forever?

What about the Roman soldiers who crucified Him? After the earthquake, it is likely that some of the soldiers said to each other, as men do today, "Let's forget about it. Let's go and get drunk. Let's drown the memories that trouble us." But the Centurion who had stood by the dying Nazarene and mused, "Surely this man must have been the Son of God" — what pathos must have gripped his soul as he realized that with his own hands he had crucified the Son of God!

What happened to the disciples that silent day? Those who had watched the crucifixion — except maybe John — watched from the far edges of the crowd. Probably they left before the rest of the crowd to save their own skins. Their Master was dead and His cause was lost. They didn't want to be crucified, too. Where did they go? Probably they headed back to that upper room where they could lock the door, just where their Master found them huddled on the first day of the week. Locked in. Hiding for fear of the Jews.

While Jesus was their Leader, they had trusted Him to stand between them and their enemies, which were also His. But now that their enemies had succeeded in killing Him, a thing they never believed could happen — what fear invaded their hearts! When the compass is lost, all landmarks become confused. Nothing goes right. The distressed disciples were tossed by storms of despair. When their Lord died, all hope died with Him.

If God is not alive, nothing else seems very important. Two of His disciples who walked the road to Emmaus the next day expressed their anguish and doubt to a stranger. "We had hoped . . .," they said, "but his death was the end of our hope."

In the Temple, ceremonies of worship continued, but the symbols had become meaningless. The priests held the usual services, made the usual sacrifices in the usual way, and tried to ignore the hastily-mended veil. The Great Sacrifice, to which all their ritual pointed, had been offered, but they did not comprehend, nor would they have admitted its potency had they been told. They put their Passover lambs on the altar, while the true Lamb of God lay in a borrowed tomb behind a sealed stone.

The Sabbath they celebrated was also dead. The New Testament Christians did not continue to worship God on Saturday. This was no day to remember, to celebrate, when the dead body of their Lord lay in a garden tomb.

Martin Luther once experienced a period of great melancholy. After several days, his wife came into his study shrouded in black, as if in mourning for the dead.

Startled, Luther turned from his desk. "Woman, who is dead?" he demanded.

"God is dead," she replied.

The great reformer laid down his pen, "My soul, he said, "why do you speak of God being dead?"

"You have been acting that way," she said, "as though all hope is gone and God is dead."

We need a resurrection of hopes that lie buried. We need a resurrection of faith that walks with a risen Saviour. We need a revival of love, a renewed grasp of the power of God just as much as did all those who somehow lived through that terrible silent Saturday when the Son of God was dead, buried in a tomb near Jerusalem.

Then another evening came. At the hour of sunset the great horns sounded from the Temple towers and the shops opened (for the Jewish calendar had a different method of reckoning). Mary Magdalene and the other women went out to buy the spices they needed to prepare for use at the tomb the next morning. After dark and through the evening hours they made preparation.

The Master didn't need their spices, but they needed the giving; they needed the occupation to make the hours bearable, to work out the duties of their faith, though their hope was gone. After times of great stress and sorrow, we all need the medicinal balm of work, the doing of which brings heartsease and healing.

The trouble with many people is that they want to avoid the work of faith. They want to sit lazily all year, being "spiritual," and then come to church on Easter and expect the resurrection to thrill their hearts. It just doesn't work that way. Anything that has been allowed to lie dormant all year isn't revived so easily.

Strange Sunday

Strange stories began circulating on the morning after the Sabbath in Jerusalem. Some whispered that Jesus of Nazareth had risen from the dead. Most people didn't even bother to wish it were true. Their reaction was, "Impossible!" Surely such a rumor was the strangest one they had ever heard, they thought.

They did not realize that this day was different from all the days that ever had been, or ever would be. To them, it was just another first day of the week. Farmers started back to their fields. In the narrow streets of Jerusalem, shopkeepers opened up for another week's business as usual. The commerce and duties of everyday life were resumed. At first, it looked the same as any other day.

But the grave that was opened caused the marts of men to close. Ever since that Sunday, the day after the Sabbath, believers in Christ have been closing up shop. On that momentous first day of the week a new age was born. Sunday became a sacred day because of what happened that particular morning. The Sabbath was dead; a new day began to be celebrated in its stead.

This day of resurrection was a day to rejoice in, and it has been ever since. "This is the day which the Lord hath made," the Psalmist said, "we will rejoice and be glad in it" (118:24). Only God could raise the dead, tear the terror from the tomb, and change fear into faith. All our rejoicing is founded on the fact that Jesus Christ became the "first-fruits" of them that sleep. We do not come to church to argue the resurrection on such a day; we come to affirm it, to celebrate it.

The followers of Jesus awoke that resurrection day with heavy hearts — if they slept at all. They did not anticipate a risen Saviour. Of all the people in the world who had to be convinced that He was alive, it was those who loved Him and had seen Him die.

Mary Magdalene and the other women made their way to

the previously-unused tomb of Joseph of Arimathaea with spices prepared to anoint a dead body. Mary's tear-blinded eyes did not recognize the significance of the empty tomb, or the marvel of a messenger from heaven, or even the Lord Himself. She was too closed-in with her grief to see the glory about her.

"Tell me where you have taken His body," she pleaded with one she thought was the gardener. He spoke her name, then, and she recognized Him joyfully, still scarcely daring to believe. She tried to hold Him, as though His nearness was a physical thing.

"Let me go," He said. As He had said to Nicodemus years before, He reaffirmed to His disciples after His resurrection, "God is a spirit: and they that worship him must worship him in spirit and in truth" (John 4:24).

We have not had the privilege of seeing Him in His risen body, but we believe that Jesus arose from the dead because of what those who saw Him wrote in the Scriptures. "For Christ also hath once suffered for sins," Peter testified, ". . . being put to death in the flesh but quickened by the Spirit" (I Peter 3:18). The apostle Paul also declared, in Romans 6:9, "Death hath no dominion over him."

A convincing evidence we have that Jesus arose from the dead is the difference it made in His disillusioned disciples. Less than forty-eight hours earlier, they had heard the last words of the Victim: "It is finished!" On the first day of the week, in the evening, they heard the words of the Victor: "It is I, be not afraid."

The continuity of the church is evidence of His resurrection. Herod sought in vain to crush the followers of Jesus. Saul the angry Pharisee sought in vain to crush the people of the Way. The Emperor of Rome martyred and scattered the Christians. Men through the ages have opposed God's Word and oppressed His church. But the Lord Jesus said, "I will build my church; and the gates of hell shall not prevail against it" (Matthew 16: 18). And they never have. Almost two thousand years later, His resurrection is heralded by His church all over the world.

On Easter, millions sing, "Up From the Grave He Arose."

On so-called "Good Friday," the Saviour was crucified by mankind. On that silent Saurday the universe held its breath to think that God was dead. But on a sublime Sunday, His resurrection proved once and for all that death was conquered. His return from the dead brought mankind a living hope, a message of good news, a new day of memorial.

On Easter, we speak of death in terms of victory. Other days we are forced to recognize death as tragedy and separation. We talk of it in hushed tones on occasions of sorrow, for death invades the homes of Christians as brutally as the homes of unbelievers. It brings grief and separation to both. The only difference is whether we meet it with faith or despair.

On Easter Day we affirm that death is defeated. We declare that it is not permanent. It can touch only the physical body, not the soul. We rejoice not only in commemorating the resurrection of our Saviour, but in anticipating that our loved ones, and we also, shall experience similar resurrection. Those who die in Christ suffer only temporary separation; the grave cannot hold them prisoner because it could not hold Him. There shall be not one bone left in the earth over which sin and Satan can claim victory.

There is so little that we can say we know about death from this side, except that it is a shattering experience, that it is the "last enemy" we have to face. But, praise God, there is a day of resurrection coming on which we will be able to say with Paul: "O death, where is thy sting? O grave, where is thy victory?" (I Corinthians 15:55).

Some blessed morning to come, the Lord Jesus, Prince and Conqueror over the tomb, shall stand as the Almighty, Preeminent One and declare that death is banished forever, as He said to John on Patmos: "I am he that liveth, and was dead; and, behold, I am alive for evermore, Amen; and have the keys of hell and of death" (Revelation 1:18). That is the glorious message of hope we can proclaim every day of the year, but especially on Easter.

7

*If in this life only we have hope
in Christ, we are of all men most
miserable. But now is Christ risen
from the dead, and become the
firstfruits of them that slept*

(I Corinthians 15:19-20).

REALITIES OF THE RESURRECTION

No concept is more universal than resurrection; none has stronger hold on the hearts of men. The idea of living on beyond the grave — perpetuation, regardless of what that is — is evidenced in all religions and cults. All men have a strong desire for continuance of life. Some of their ideas about a future life are very lofty, but some of them are very base in nature.

All of us find it difficult to accept the idea of death. One author titled her book with a cry of desperation, "I Want to Live!" and created a best seller, because it captured the imagination.

The hunger for immortality is strong in the breast of every man. Some are able to adjust to the idea of death with the concept of reincarnation. Some Eastern mystics teach another life on this earth in some other substance: perhaps a tree, or an animal, or another person — but living again, somehow.

When we, as Christians, speak of resurrection, we deal with

an idea altogether different from those reflected in other religions. For us, everything we believe — and our whole future — depends upon the reality of the resurrection of Jesus Christ.

Long before Jesus lived on earth, Greek philosophers discussed the immortality of the soul. Their emphasis was on beauty of life and thought — the perpetuation of personal influence, in which a man's name is remembered and his good thoughts and deeds live on. This may be true, but it is not enough. The Bible does say that our works follow us — that is, they have influence on others even after we are dead. But the Greek philosophers believed that when the grave was closed, life was ended except for the influence that lingered in the memory of others.

Many modern men also hold the concept that there is nothing more after the grave — only annihilation.

In attempting to discuss resurrection, or immortality, immediately we have to settle the question as to whether our basis is philosophy or the New Testament. Jesus taught and exemplified a different concept of life after death. We must define what resurrection is — especially His resurrection.

Some say the resurrection of Jesus was only a spiritual resurrection, that He did not actually come forth from the grave, and that our resurrection will also be in spirit and not in body. Spiritually, Jesus never died in the first place — nobody does, except the death of sin, the "second death." Men die only physically. Jesus gave up His spirit, which left His physical body. Then His body was declared dead and buried in a grave.

What does the word *resurrection* mean? Going back to the original language of the New Testament, the English word *resurrection* is translated from Greek words which mean "up" or "again" — "caused to stand" or "to be raised up again." The Scriptures teach that the individual at the resurrection shall *stand up*; he will arise from the grave to live again.

The Bible indicates that a person lives for eternity in a conscious, visible, tangible, recognizable body. When a person dies, the body returns to dust — we plant it in the ground tenderly and reverently, leaving it to await the resurrection. Whether the person is a believer or a non-believer, there is no such thing as "soul-sleep." The soul does not go into the grave, but goes at the moment of death to the proper dwelling-place of that soul, whether it be heaven or hell — the choice having already been made and the destiny fixed.

Admittedly, it leaves us with some questions we cannot answer. Sometimes I wish that we could be translated like Elijah of the Old Testament. If we were the men that Elijah and Enoch were, maybe we might be. But God had sent for them when He was through with them, and their bodies never did see corruption. They never did go to the dust of the earth.

It would be so easy to echo the philosophy of the spiritual which says,

> I looked over Jordan, and what did I see,
> Comin' for to carry me home?
> A band of angels comin' after me,
> Comin' for to carry me home.

When the apostle Paul preached in Athens, the Greeks wanted to know what he thought about immortality. "Ye men of Athens," he began his sermon, "in all things I perceive that ye are very religious" (Acts 17:22, a.s.v.).

"What is your religion more than ours?" they wanted to know. "What does it offer?"

The most distinctive thing Christianity has to offer is the blessed hope of life beyond the grave. And belief about the future has a lot to do with behavior in the present. "If in this life only we have hope in Christ," Paul wrote in another place, "we are of all men most miserable" (I Corinthians 15:19).

The experiences of those Old Testament saints like Enoch and Elijah who never died, but were translated, will not be duplicated except by those who are alive when Jesus comes. They did not experience death as our loved ones who have gone on have known it. But we cannot tell the translation of these Old Testament characters "resurrection."

Several people were raised in the Old Testament whose return from the dead is more accurately described by the word *resuscitation* — a reviving again to life from the dead.

Revival of Many

Those who were translated or raised in the Old Testament, or even those who were raised by Christ in the New Testament, had an experience different from that of Christ Himself. They came back to life only to die again. Their experience is best described as "revival from the dead." They came back to life only to die again. And that is a vast difference.

During a famine, the prophet Elijah was fed by a widow. Later on, when her son died, Elijah took her boy up to his chamber and laid him down on the bed. He covered the boy's body with his own three times and prayed to God. Then the dead lad came back to life. This was not a resurrection like Christ's, for the boy had to die again, eventually. Some feel that Elijah simply used artificial respiration. You can call it whatever you want, but the Bible says that the boy was dead and he lived again (I Kings 17:21-22).

Many years later, a soldier of Israel died in battle. His friends could not bury him as they wished because of pressure from the enemy, so they threw his body into a cave nearby. It happened to be where Elisha the prophet had been buried some years before. "When the man was let down," the Bible says, "and touched the bones of Elisha, he revived, and stood up on his feet" (II Kings 13:21). No artificial respiration here; when the body of the dead soldier fell upon the bones of Elisha, he was revived from the dead. The soldier was alive to fight again, perhaps — and to die again.

In the New Testament, the story of Jairus' daughter is a familiar one. The father had gone to get Jesus to cure her illness, but before they reached Jairus' home, the girl died. Jesus went into the upper room, took the small hand and said, "Maid, arise. And her spirit came again, and she arose straightway; and he commanded to give her meat" (Luke 8:54-55). She was revived from the dead, but it was not resurrection. She was raised up to eat and play, and perhaps to grow up — but she had to die again.

Jesus saw a weeping widow walking by the bier of her only son to bury him. The Lord went over and looked down at the body and said, "Young man, I say unto thee, Arise. And he that was dead sat up, and began to speak. And he delivered him to his mother" (Luke 7:14-15). He was revived from the dead — he got off his bier to talk and walk and embrace his mother — but he was alive only to die again.

When Lazarus died, Jesus waited four days, knowing that if He came earlier, His enemies might say Lazarus had just swooned. But after the body had been buried four days, everyone knew that he was truly dead. Then Jesus "cried with a loud voice, Lazarus, come forth. And he that was dead came forth . . ." (John 11:43-44).

Lazarus walked out of his cave-tomb, had his gravewrappings removed, and later feasted with his friends. But it was not resurrection, it was revival of the dead, for Lazarus died again. I have visited his grave; I have touched the headstone.

In the history of the early church, a woman named Dorcas was beloved by her church because of her good works. When she died, her friends sent for Peter and said, "Please do something!" How we wish, often, that we could "do something" for those in sorrow!

"All the widows stood by him weeping, and showing the coats and garments which Dorcas made, while she was with them." It would be a grand thing if we had done enough work in our lifetimes that people would miss us, wouldn't it? Simon Peter prayed; and turning to the body said, "Tabitha, arise." She opened her eyes, and when she saw Peter, she sat up. (Acts 9:39-40). She went back to work for the church like she always had — but eventually she had to die again.

While Paul was preaching on the second floor of a house at Troas, a young man sitting in an open window went to sleep "and fell down from the third loft, and was taken up dead. And Paul went down and fell on him, and embracing him said, . . . his life is in him. . . . And they brought the young man alive. . . ." (Acts 20:9-12). This was another revival from the dead, but not a resurrection, for the young man had to die again.

Resurrection of Jesus

The resurrection of Jesus was unique. It was different from all these other incidents. He was the only One who ever died and arose of Himself, never to die again. He was buried in a sealed tomb, but on the third day He came forth by His own power.

After Jesus arose from the dead, His disciples could see Him, converse with Him, and touch Him. They watched Him break bread and eat fish. He had a tangible body. He had, also, a transcendent body, which went through barred doors into the upper room.

On the cross, Jesus cried out, "Father, into Thy hands I commend My spirit," and His spirit went home to God.

The servants of Nicodemus and Joseph of Arimathaea didn't take down from the cross His spirit, but His earthly tabernacle, the body of clay. The seed of Eve, and Abraham, and David, in which the Second Person of the Trinity had lived for a little while. They didn't bury the spirit of Jesus, but only His body. Therefore, when He arose, His spirit came back from God to dwell again in that body.

Jesus rose from the grave in a glorified body — but do not therefore presume that immortality and resurrection are the same. Immortality may be the speculation of philosophers; bodily resurrection is the guarantee of immortality in the New Testament, and it is inseparably linked with the forgiveness of our sins: "If Christ be not raised," the apostle Paul wrote, "your faith is vain, ye are yet in your sins" (I Corinthians 15: 17).

When the women, Peter, and John returned from the tomb that morning with the incredible news that Jesus had risen from the dead, it seemed too good to be true. It was indeed the strangest story ever told.

They scarcely believed it themselves; certainly they did not fully comprehend it beforehand. When He was transfigured before three of His disciples, He charged them, "Tell no man of this." If they had, who would have believed them? They themselves could scarcely believe it was not a dream. Even though they had a "sneak preview" of His resurrection glory, they couldn't really believe that He had risen until they saw Him themselves.

After the resurrection, strange stories circulated around Jerusalem and triggered different reactions in the people who heard that the body of Jesus was no longer in His tomb.

"He is dead!" the priests insisted. "We saw Him die." And immediately the leaders of the Jews began to establish lies to account for the missing body. They instructed the guards to say that Jesus' disciples had stolen it away.

Some people, even today, insist that He must have swooned on the cross, and not really died. Then when He was put into the tomb, the coolness revived Him and He regained consciousness.

That would not have convinced the Roman soldiers whose duty it was to crucify prisoners. They had watched Jesus die. The seasoned centurion had been ordered to break His bones that He might die more quickly — but he was already dead. To be sure, they thrust a spear into His side. Nobody could convince the Romans that Jesus had not actually died on the cross.

The disciples did not doubt His death. When Mary said she had seen Him and talked with Him, they didn't believe her. They simply could not believe that He was alive until He came into that upper room and they saw Him for themselves. Thomas, who was absent the first time He appeared insisted, "I will not believe unless I see in His hands the print of the nails!"

The words of the angel who stood by the tomb were unmistakable: "Fear not, for I know that ye seek Jesus, who was crucified. He is not here, for he is risen, as he said. Come, see the place where the Lord lay" (Matthew 28:5-6).

What difference does the resurrection make? Those disciples, who on Friday evening were scattered, every man for himself, left the watching to women waiting in the shadows. Only two rich and powerful secret disciples were brave enough to ask Pilate for His body, and there weren't enough of the twelve around to be pall-bearers. For two days and nights they huddled behind locked doors, fearful for their lives. They had hoped Jesus would free them from Roman oppression, but the Romans had crucified Him. All had been in vain!

Only a few weeks later, Peter spoke forth boldly in Jerusalem, saying, "God hath made that same Jesus, whom ye have crucified, both Lord and Christ" (Acts 2:36). That day many thousand were won to faith in Christ. Each of the eleven disciples finally died a martyr for His cause — they knew they had a hope worth dying for. They preached the gospel regardless of opposition. It was the resurrection that made the difference!

Stephen, the first martyr, stood boldly before the Sanhedrin and declared Jesus was "the Just One, of whom ye have been now the betrayers and murderers" (Acts 7:52).

Mere loyalty, even to a good and holy man, does not create such boldness and power. Their Master who had died was alive again, ascended on high where nothing could ever touch Him. And through His power, nothing could touch them — even death but hastened them into His glorious presence.

There was another occurrence along with the crucifixion and resurrection of Jesus which is often overlooked. It is one of the most supernatural happenings in all the New Testament. On the day Jesus died, crying with a loud voice as He gave up His spirit, in Jerusalem the veil of the Temple was torn from top to bottom, and the earth quaked. "And the graves were opened; and many bodies of the saints which slept arose. And came out of the graves after His resurrection, and went into the holy city, and appeared unto many" (Matthew 27:52-53).

Evidently the graves stayed open until the first day of the week, the bodies exposed. The Sabbath was a holy day, and to have touched the graves or the bodies would have made the Jews ceremonially unclean and contaminated. They did not come forth until after the resurrection of Jesus. Then they were seen by many, perhaps their own families and friends. They were the first to experience the power of His resurrection, but all who believe on Him will rise, likewise, when He comes again.

It is not possible to explain away the resurrection of Jesus. Every doubter and atheist has to live with this great fact of history! Jesus was seen after His resurrection by His eleven disciples, and also by a crowd of over five hundred. And "last of all," Paul says, "he was seen of me, as of one born out of due time" (I Corinthians 15:8).

The resurrection of Jesus was like no other; His was the true, the initial resurrection, the hope of glory for the saints of all ages. Theory is not enough; we need the hope exemplified in the resurrection of the Lord Jesus Christ.

Raising of All

The Bible teaches that all men will be raised from the dead: the believer and the unbeliever, the just and the unjust. Every man shall come forth from the grave — from the depths of the sea, from the bowels of the earth, from the outer reaches of the air. God is not going to let death have the victory over a single bone. He will reach down and bring forth all the dead. The resurrection of Jesus Christ was an imperative: "For as in Adam all die, even so in Christ (the second Adam) shall all be made alive" (I Corinthians 15:22). "I am the resurrection and the life," Jesus said, "He that believeth in me, though he were dead, yet shall he live" (John 11:25). As Jesus arose from the tomb, we have the hope that we also shall come forth from the grave. Together with those of our loved ones who die in the Lord, we shall be caught up together to meet the Lord when He comes.

There is certainly a resurrection of the just and a resurrection of the unjust. "And many of them that sleep in the dust of the earth shall awake: Some to everlasting life, and some to shame and everlasting contempt" (Daniel 12:2). Then we find again where Jesus said, "And thou shalt be blessed; for they cannot recompense thee; for thou shalt be recompensed at the resurrection of the just" (Luke 14:14). When will these resurrections be? It does not matter so much whether it is a thousand years from now or today — it is going to happen.

Occasionally, upon approaching an Easter Sunday when the church will be full, I wonder if I should not preach on the resurrection of the unjust. Somehow many seem to believe that the resurrection will make everything all right. But if it isn't all right when we die, it will not be all right with us on the resurrection day. Destiny has already been determined. Some will be raised to reunion and reward but some to shame and contempt and everlasting torment.

A great English preacher of the last century, F. B. Meyer, had a devoted preacher friend — but each was busy with his own work. They corresponded once in a while, saying, "We must get together!" Finally, when Dr. Meyer became ill and recognized that his life's sun was sinking fast, he wrote to his friend, "It looks like we will not get together here. But I do so hope that God will do us the favor of putting our cottages close together in heaven so that we can talk everything over."

There will be a great reunion of believers in heaven. But most glorious of all, we will see God and our Lord Jesus Christ.

A small town doctor knew the boy he was treating was fatally ill, but for a few weeks the boy became stronger and went back to Sunday School once or twice. Then he had to be put to bed again.

"Will I be able to go to Sunday School next Sunday?" the boy asked the doctor.

Knowing the child did not understand that his illness was something only the Great Physician could heal, the doctor asked, "Son, why is it so important that you go to Sunday School next Sunday?"

"My Sunday School teacher has been telling us about the tabernacle," the boy said. "She made us a picture, and next Sunday she is going to take us behind the veil and show us where God was."

The doctor turned away so that the child could not see his face. "I am sure," he said, "that next Sunday you will see where God is."

When the trumpet of God sounds and the voice of God speaks — the implication here is of a military command that cannot be disobeyed — it will be taps for the unsaved. But it will be reveille for the saved — that golden daybreak when Jesus shall come.

Those who have died before will not be slighted: ". . . the dead in Christ shall rise first," Paul wrote. "Then we which are alive and remain shall be caught up together with them in the clouds, to meet the Lord in the air: and so shall we ever be with the Lord" (I Thessalonians 4:16-17).

Where will we be? We will be with Jesus, and that is all that is important. There is not a grave that will not one day be opened; never a body has breathed but it will be resurrected.

8

And when he had spoken these things, while they beheld, he was taken up; and a cloud received him out of their sight

(Acts 1:9).

ASSURANCES OF THE ASCENSION

The crowning moment of Jesus' first advent was His ascension! It demonstrated that God acknowledged His Son in receiving Him back into heaven.

Some of us make far too little of the ascension of Jesus. Checking my library, I find very few sermons on it. Not many preachers have preached on the ascension. We are so happy about the resurrection that it is tempting to stop there. But the Lord stayed on earth for about six weeks after His resurrection. Surely there was a purpose in this great climactic moment.

What did the Lord say to us in His ascension? His resurrection was unique; it was reserved only for Him who was the Son of God. More fully comprehending the power and glory of His resurrection, we recognize that it proved beyond any shadow of doubt that He was the Son of God.

The scene on the Mount of Olives, as described in the Bible, shows man's view of the triumphant return of the Son of God to heaven to sit down at the right hand of the throne of God. "For he must reign, till he hath put all enemies under his feet" (I Corinthians 15:25).

Jesus stood at the watershed of history. More than any other, He could truly say, "I came, I saw, I conquered." He did not leave unfinished any task that God assigned Him on earth. Every foundation of redemption, every provision for our salvaton, every miracle of attestation — everything that God had in mind for the Son to do was accomplished. Therefore Jesus could return and sit down in triumph at the right hand of His Father. Christ conquered sin in the wilderness, death on the cross, hell in the grave, and all the forces of evil in space as He ascended from the earth into the presence of His Father.

It is not easy to summarize all He did during the thirty-three years of His life. Behind Him stood the barn of Bethlehem; beyond Him beckoned the heavenly mansions not made with hands. Behind Him our vale of tears, beyond Him the heights of Glory. Behind Him the persecution of men, beyond Him the applause of angels. Behind Him the garden of grief, beyond Him the realm of Glory where He will reign forever. Behind Him old Jerusalem, beyond Him the New Jerusalem.

John, on the Isle of Patmos, said he was caught up in the Spirit and "saw the holy city, new Jerusalem, coming down from God out of heaven, prepared as a bride adorned for her husband" (Revelation 21:2). Behind Jesus stood the gory hill of Calvary, beyond Him loomed the glory land of heaven. Behind Him the cross and beyond Him the crown. The ascension was the complete and perfect climax to all Christ's earthly ministry. It demonstrated His Lordship.

The greatest miracle in the life of Christ was His ascension into heaven. He was lifted up publicly in the presence of perhaps five hundred or more people. They watched Him incredulously. Could such a thing be possible? He ascended up into the sky without any sign of assistance. Redemption was completed and God received Him back into His presence as His own Son. Some of those who watched His ascension had difficulty in believing it.

There are those today, also, who have difficulty in believing the miracles of Jesus. Why such a problem? Go to any airport and watch a plane that weighs more than five tons lift itself into the air. If man's engineering can create such a thing, why should not God be able to lift the body of His Son and receive Him into Glory?

Our God is able to do miracles! We have some hints of the pattern in the Old Testament. In ancient times, "Enoch walked with God: and he was not; for God took him" (Genesis 5:24). A little child put the story beautifully: "Enoch walked and talked with God often, and one day he was closer to God's house than he was to his own, so God said, 'Just come on home with me.'" The same pattern is there; God took Enoch unto Himself.

Moses died on the mountain overlooking the Promised Land and God buried Him — where, no man knows. God was the undertaker and the only pallbearer; He presided at the service and laid Moses to rest. For Moses had completed the service God had commissioned him on earth.

When Elijah was through with his work, God sent angels with a chariot of fire that took Elijah up out of the sight of Elisha. But Jesus went home in a glorified body.

The body of man has been a puzzle to many people. Ever since the very beginning, when Adam and Eve disobeyed God and experienced sin, mankind has had to die. In death, the human body no longer responds; it no longer functions, no longer moves, no longer breathes. The first time Adam and Eve looked upon a person who was dead, they did not know what to think of it — any more than we know today, for all our scientific achievements. According to the first indications in the Scriptures, man had been dead spiritually for nine hundred years before they had to deal with a body that was dead physically.

Jesus' body was buried. Yet He arose with a resurrected body in which He ascended into heaven. This is the first example of the kind of bodies we will have in our heavenly home. Enoch was taken to be with God without suffering death — we do not know how. God sent angels with a chariot of fire for Elijah. But Jesus didn't need any guide or helper to get to heaven. He knew where He was going; He knew where His Father was, because He had lived there from before the foundation of the world. He simply returned to His home in glory.

Forty Days

Jesus remained and ministered on earth for forty days after He came out of the tomb. Why did He, in the language of the street, "hang around" forty days? Had not the world hurt Him enough? Had not men tried to destroy Him? Had they not rejected Him? Why did He stay on earth after His resurrection?

We should not disregard these forty days, for there is more written in the Scriptures about this period than about the first thirty years of Jesus' life. The forty-day period was full of mystery, blessed fellowship, and startling phenomena.

The number "forty" occurs often in the Bible. The Israelites wandered in the wilderness forty years; Elijah journeyed to Horeb forty days. Jesus fasted in the wilderness forty days and He stayed upon earth forty days after His resurrection. It is food for thought that the days of His testing and temptation were equal to His days upon earth after His resurrection from the dead.

Why did He stay? To teach the disciples — and to teach us some things, also. Those days made a difference in the lives of His disciples. Every time Jesus had mentioned death to them, they shrank from it — just as you and I shrink from it. Many families neglect to discuss arrangements; when the stark reality of death hits them in the face, they cannot think clearly, simply because all of their lives they have blocked it out. When Jesus tried to talk of death, His disciples wouldn't listen. When He said He had to go to Jerusalem to die, they argued, "Be it far from thee, Lord" (Matthew 16:22). But Jesus steadfastly set His face toward Jerusalem.

"Let not your heart be troubled," He said to them, ". . . ye believe in God, believe also in me. In my Father's house are many mansions . . . ." (John 14:1-2).

"Lord, we know not where thou goest," Thomas protested, "and how can we know the way?"

"Lord, don't go away from us," they begged. "If You leave us, we will not know how to get along!" Separation is always difficult.

Joseph Parker, a great London preacher had some peculiarities. One of them was that when he and his wife married, he made a promise that he would never say "goodbye" on any occasion. When they visited in a home, he would often leave abruptly, not taking a formal departure. He just could not stand to say "goodbye" to anyone. The disciples had something of the same problem. They didn't want the Lord to say "goodbye"; they wanted Him to stay with them.

But after He ascended into heaven, the Scriptures say, they "returned to Jerusalem with great joy" (Luke 24:52) from the Mount of Olives. What changed them? They had learned, in these forty days, to love Jesus in the right fashion. Before, they had loved Him mostly for what He could do for them. I fear we also love Him much of the time for the same reason. Many people seem to think of God only as a convenient burden-bearer, because He is "a very present help in trouble" (Psalm 46:1).

His disciples were happy that Jesus was going back to His Father and their Father. They were happy that He was going to prepare a place for them. They realized that He had done what He came to do, and that it was all for them. Now they were happy that He was going to work through them.

"Lord, we don't want you to get away from us," we plead. "If you do, the burdens of life become unbearable."

I wish you and I could learn something here — at least that we would not use the phrase "doing church work." If our work isn't for the glory of God, if it isn't joyful, if we don't come to the Lord's house because of the precious things available there, then God help us! We are wrong to think of the

Son of God always working *for* us, although He is. We need to pray, "Lord, work *through* us."

Flesh or Spirit?

There is a difference between flesh and spirit, especially in the work of the Lord. For thirty-three years Jesus lived in a physical body; now He lives in a glorified body — but it is still a real body. The life of Jesus during His earthly ministry, prior to His crucifixion, is spoken of as "the days of his flesh" (Hebrews 5:7).

When Jesus came into the upper room, He had come through a locked door, and yet His presence made an impression on their physical senses: seeing, hearing, touching, feeling — so that they would be convinced that it was He.

Thomas said he would not believe the Lord was risen unless he could handle Him. Therefore Jesus appeared to them again when Thomas was present and challenged him to "Reach hither thy finger and behold my hands" (John 20:27). He had a transcendent body, but it was undeniably recognizable — touchable flesh, yet glorified.

The Scriptures say that He appeared first to Mary Magdalene, out of whom He had cast seven devils. How much she needed His comfort! Jesus spoke to her tenderly.

When Mary recognized Him, she grabbed His feet desperately, as much as to say, "It's been so terrible, not knowing whether I'd ever see you again. Never again will you get away!"

"Touch me not," Jesus said to her, "for I am not yet ascended to my Father." She couldn't hold on to Him. The physical body is not the important thing. We need to remember that when we come down to the last moments of life. Jesus says to us, "Don't try to hold on to the earthly tabernacle as though it were all of life!"

Although Peter had cursed and denied his Master, the angel said to the women, "But go your way, tell his disciples *and*

Peter . . ." (Mark 16:7). It was the best news Simon had ever heard, that the Lord still cared about him.

By the sea of Galilee, Jesus came to the edge of the water and called out to the disciples in the boat, saying, "Children, have ye any meat?" (John 21:5). They rushed back to the shore. The nail-scarred hands of Jesus reached for one of the raw fish, cooked it over the fire and ate it in their presence.

Fact or Fantasy?

Are His resurrection and ascension facts or fantasies, then? The fact of His glorious return to His Father is mentioned thirty-three times in the New Testament.

Here we are not dealing with a tricky master magician. We are dealing with the reality of the Son of God. You have to accept His honesty, or you have to call Him only a clever man, who misled His followers. What did the sight of their Lord ascending do for His disciples and the others? It turned cowards into the bravest of men.

What about the three who saw Him even later? The dying Stephen looked up into heaven, saw Jesus standing to welcome him and cried out, "Lord Jesus, receive my spirit" (Acts 7:59). Stephen was able to die because he saw a vision of the ascended Christ.

Paul was converted on the road to Damascus when heaven opened and the Lord appeared to him. "Who art thou, Lord?" the proud Pharisee named Saul of Tarsus asked — humbly, I think.

"I am Jesus, whom thou persecutest," was the reply (Acts 9: 5). The zealous persecutor of Christians was converted because of his vision of the ascended Christ.

In the first chapter of Revelation, we find that John, on the Isle of Patmos, was "in the Spirit on the Lord's day" and saw "the Son of man" high and lifted up. His description of the ascended Christ is one of the most magnificent in human literature. The vision gave John power to write the Lord's message to the seven churches of Asia Minor declaring, "I am Alpha and Omega, the beginning and the ending, saith the Lord, who is, and who was, and who is to come, the Almighty" (Revelation 1:8).

John was exiled to this island while his people back on the mainland were undergoing persecution. He never knew how it was with them, whether they were able to withstand the temptation and the pressures. It is likely that he went every morning to scan the ocean for a ship. When John began to describe heaven, he said, "I saw a new heaven and a new earth; . . . and there was no more sea" (Revelation 21:1).

What did the sea represent? Separation. John heard the roaring of the sea and the tide coming in and going out day after day and night after night. "When I get to heaven," he thought, "I'll not be separated from those I love by the sea." Only the vision of the ascended Christ gave John power to endure patiently.

Why didn't Jesus slip away quietly, instead of ascending publicly? It was because He was baptized publicly, crucified publicly, and buried publicly. Therefore He ascended publicly. He had nothing to hide. Everything that He did was a matter of public record.

After His resurrection, Jesus stayed on to identify Himself more clearly as the Son of God. He stayed on to comfort His disciples. "It is expedient for you that I go away," He told them. They were depending on Him too much. One wrote to the Hebrew Christians later: "For . . . ye . . . are become such as have need of milk, and not of strong meat" (5:12).

It was time for them to grow up, time they were making decisions, time they carried the burdens. "It is needful for you!"

Jesus returned to heaven, therefore, to sit down at the right hand of God. He is standing in the presence of God, interceding for us. He is our advocate.

There was another reason for His going away that we may have missed: it was needful that He go away because in the

Old Testament the priest went behind the curtain into the Holy of Holies to put the blood of the sacrifice upon the Mercy Seat.

Jesus' death had been the sacrifice for the whole world. When He was through with His earthly ministry, when He had done everything needful in the outside court of the tabernacle, He went behind the curtain of God, into the holy presence of God. It was needful for us that He go away because He was our High Priest. "Wherefore in all things it behooved Him to be made like unto his brethren, that he might be a merciful and faithful high priest in things pertaining to God, to make reconciliation for the sins of the people" (Hebrews 2:17). He went back to glory to take His eternal sin-offering to the Father.

The ascension of Jesus is proof of His deity. A cloud came down and He was received into it. The cloud was "God's Ascension Special." On it, Jesus went back to the glory He had with His Father before the world was. Yet He returned there in the form of a man, assuring us a place in heaven with Him.

Admiral Nelson, perhaps the most famous of all British naval men, was very daring. With his small group of vessels he pursued halfway around the world an enemy fleet twice as large and well-fitted as his. In a letter back to England, one of his captains wrote, "We are half starved. We are dead on our feet. We don't understand all of the journey. But we are more than recompensed to know that we are with Nelson."

When we get to heaven, we will be more than recompensed in being with Christ. The toils of the road will seem nothing! "And I will pray the Father," He promised, "and he shall give you another Comforter, that he may abide with you for ever" (John 14:16). We may be lonely, but we are never really alone — Jesus promised never to leave us alone.

When Jesus went beyond the skies to His Father, it demonstrated that He was God's Son. No one else could so defy the laws of nature. Satan would have stopped him. God wouldn't have received him. But He was the exalted Son of God who had finished His redeeming work on earth. In His hands, He bore the sin offering for the whole world; He had made provision for all that were His. The Scripture was fulfilled that "he led captivity captive, and gave gifts unto men" (Ephesians 4:8).

Having in our hearts the assurance of His presence with us, knowing the joy of His triumphal return to His Father, let us serve our risen Saviour with gladness in the power of His Holy Spirit.

9

I will make darkness light before them, and crooked things straight. These things will I do unto them and not forsake them

(Isaiah 42:16).

VOICE OF THE VICTOR

What does serving a risen, ascended, victorious Christ mean to you? Are you always conscious that the victory is the Lord's? Do you feel certain that faith and hope will prevail? Can you hear the voice of God and know that He is able to meet all difficulties?

We pass through many crises in life — personal, economic, natural. We often feel that because the world around us changes, and we change, we wonder if God changes, too. Does God still have the power today He did in Old Testament times? Can He still work mighty miracles? Can He still bring revival to the hearts of men? Is He able to remake communities, challenge churches, and revitalize our spiritual lives so that living seems really worthwhile?

When Jesus was on His way to the cross, soldiers guarded Him. Many spectators likely did not know Him; they only noticed another man going to his death. This trail to Golgotha had been used many times by the Roman soldiers. Some who sympathized followed at a distance; those who loved Jesus weeping out their travail.

"Weep not for me," the Master said, "but weep for yourselves, and for your children" (Luke 23:28). The Saviour never lost faith in God's victory! He knew that He was in the will of God. "He shall not cry, nor lift up, nor cause his voice to be heard in the street" declared an Old Testament prophet (Isaiah 42:2). His death was not an accident; the enmity of the whole world could not kill Him unless His Father willed it. His death was not waste, but victory!

As the soldiers came to break the legs of those crucified to hasten their deaths, when they came to Jesus they said, "He is dead already." It was as much as to say, "He is finished!" But they had not been listening closely: earlier He had said, "It is finished!"

"*It* is finished" — the redemptive work that He came to do, *it* was finished! His words were not a whimper, nor an apology, but a victorious shout! It was a song of the Saviour, for He turned His face toward heaven, after the darkness, and lifted up His voice, "Father, into thy hands I commend my spirit!" What he had been sent to do was completed. Men thought that Jesus of Nazareth was finished, but no! "*It* is finished!"

Men have to reevaluate history because the grave did not finish Him. No other man ever went into the grave and came forth again. When a man asked Talleyrand how he could get a following to start a new religion, he was answered, "There is one plan which you might at least try. I should recommend that you get yourself crucified and rise again the third day."

Jesus did just that. Because He was victorious over the grave, lies had to be concocted. The priests claimed that someone had come and stolen His body away. Down through the centuries, some have tried to say that He was not dead rather than admit that the impossible happened; this was the only grave that was not victorious over the body placed in it.

When Napoleon was winning victory after victory across Europe, his voice and presence gave zeal and spirit to his troops: "Your emperor is with you!" was all he had to say to them. But when he was defeated at Waterloo, he was no longer able to inspire his troops. Alexander the Great conquered the known world with his army, but after he died, his army disintegrated.

Charlemagne met death in battle and was no longer a victor. He demanded, as his last request, that he be buried in an upright position in his grave, because he wanted to be in a position of command, not of helplessness. Years later, when the grave was opened, on the scroll that had slipped from his hands were the words, "What shall it profit a man if he gain the whole world, and lose his own soul?" (Mark 8:36).

If you want to gain the world, Jesus said, you must lose yourself. He came into the world, born of a humble maiden, cradled in a manger. He walked the paths of Palestine all the way to the cross in order that He might lose Himself into the lives of His people. Some have said that He was a failure: He never traveled far, He never owned real estate, He was never acclaimed by men. He was condemned, despised, and rejected. In what way could you say that this Man was triumphant?

What Does the Father Say?

He was a successful Saviour, because the Father said, "This is my beloved Son: hear ye him" (Mark 9:7). Regardless of what the world has to say, God's applause is more important than anything else.

"The Father and I are one," Jesus claimed. "I am in the Father, and the Father in me" (John 14:10). When a disciple asked, "Lord, show us the Father," the Master chided, "Have I been so long time with you, and yet hast thou not known me, Philip? He that hath seen me hath seen the Father" (John 14:9).

The Father testified also to His identification with Jesus Christ. At the beginning of the Lord's earthly ministry, Jesus went down into the baptismal waters. As He came out, a Dove came down from the opened heavens and a Voice spoke from heaven saying, "This is my beloved Son, in whom I am well pleased" (Matthew 3:17). There was no doubt in the minds of those who stood by the River Jordan. These were not the words of John the Baptist. This was a Voice from up higher.

Most of the religious leaders of the Jews had a different opinion of Jesus and His claims. "He hath spoken blasphemy!" declared the High Priest. "What further need have we of witnesses? Behold, now ye have heard his blasphemy" (Matthew 26:65).

When Jesus drew near the end of His ministry and the cross loomed immediately in front of Him, the mighty Voice from heaven came again on the Mount of Transfiguration. His three astonished disciples were commanded, "This is my beloved Son, hear him!"

Was Jesus successful? Teachers admit that Jesus was in truth a master teacher. Men dedicated to medicine say that Jesus' healing touch was beyond that of any man; He was truly the Great Physician. Any sane king that ever walked the face of the earth would bow and put his crown at Jesus' feet, saying, "Thou art the King of kings and Lord of Lords."

Jesus Himself said, "The Father that sent me beareth witness of me" (John 8:18).

Whom Do Men Say That I Am?

Jesus was vastly interested in what men had to say about Him. He turned to His disciples on one occasion and asked, "Whom do men say that I, the Son of man, am?"

"John the Baptist: but some say, Elias; and others, one of the prophets," His disciples answered.

"But whom do ye say that I am?" Jesus persisted.

Simon Peter, voicing what he felt in his heart, the hope and faith of the years he had walked with the Master, said, "Thou art the Christ, the Son of the living God" (Matthew 16:16).

There is no place to hide yourself from the Son of God. He is inescapable. "Before Abraham was, I am," He declared (John 8:58). He is still asking men today, "Who do you say that I am?" You are witness to the world what you believe about God.

At the foot of the cross, some of the spectators acted as though Jesus were eternally dead. Some live today as though Jesus did not rise from the dead and God would never demand judgment. But the voice of the Victor one day will claim this world as His own, and the judgment of God will come to all who have rejected Him.

He who is to be the Judge of all the earth stood silently before Pilate, the Roman governor, to find out what the courts of the world would say about Him. Pilate hesitated. From the secular point of view, there is no reason why the cynical Roman should suddenly have developed a conscience — except that for the first time he realized that he was in the presence of a man who was completely innocent. Some of us might not be guilty of things with which we are charged, but all of us know that we are guilty of something, somewhere, sometime. In the sight of all men, Jesus' character was flawless, as became the Son of God He claimed to be. There was no fault found in Him.

Pilate, because of the insistence of his wife, because of the probing of his conscience, turned to the multitude and said, "I find no fault in this man." This is the only time in all history that any duly appointed officer has ever said, "I believe the man who stands before me is absolutely and completely faultless."

What Does God's Record Say?

More than what the courts would say and more than what men would say, we want to know what the record of God says. For did not Jesus claim to be the long-awaited Messiah, the Saviour of men?

What does God's Word say about Him? The apostle John started his account of the life of the Lord with the statement that ". . . the Word became flesh and dwelt among us" (John 1:14). He is the everlasting Christ, the Word of God. "There is no other name under heaven given among men, whereby we must be saved," Peter declared to the Sanhedrin with surprising boldness (Acts 4:12).

Jesus' ministry was one of teaching, healing, preaching. God instructed Jesus' disciples, "Hear ye Him!" Hear Jesus, for He is the only one who can mend hearts and change lives.

What does the voice of the Victor say? "Come unto me," Jesus besought those who doubted and were discouraged, "all ye that labor and are heavy laden, and I will give you rest" (Matthew 11:28). Through Jesus, God is hearable.

"Heaven and earth shall pass away," Jesus declared, "but my words shall not pass away" (Matthew 24:35). God is durable! He gave us, not a monument, but a Man — the Son of man who is also the Son of God. Everything else shall pass away.

We live in a changing, turbulent society, but God remains unchanging. The Bible says, "Jesus Christ, the same yesterday, and today, and for ever" (Hebrews 13:8). "This is my beloved Son," God said. "Hear Him!"

Hear what Jesus has to say concerning the devil: ". . . it is written, "Thou shalt not tempt the Lord thy God . . . Get thee hence, Satan" (Matthew 4:7, 10). Just before the cross, Jesus said to Peter, "Satan hath desired to have you, that he may sift you as wheat" (Luke 22:31). But as the apostle Paul wrote, "There hath no temptation taken you but such as is common to man; but God is faithful, who . . . will with the temptation, also make a way of escape" (I Corinthians 10:13).

Then what does the voice of the Victor say to those who are defeated? The apostle Paul wrote under the inspiration of the Holy Spirit, "And we know that all things work together for good to them that love God" (Romans 8:28). Then Paul added, "Who shall separate us from the love of Christ? Shall tribulation, or distress, or persecution, or famine, or nakedness, or peril, or sword? . . . Nay, in all these things we are more than conquerors through him that loved us" (Romans 8:35, 37). This does not sound like an uncertain voice; this sounds like the authoritative voice of God, who has the power of this world in His hands.

"But what does He have to say about death?" you may ask. Jesus didn't say much about death — He conquered it rather than talked about it. But the apostle Paul wrote, "When this corruptible shall have put on incorruption, and this mortal shall have put on immortality, then shall be brought to pass the saying that is written, Death is swallowed up in victory. . . . Thanks be to God who giveth us the victory through our Lord Jesus Christ" (I Corinthians 15:54, 57).

Jesus conquered death and one day, through Him, we shall also be victorious over the grave. As long as we live in this physical body, death will threaten us, but the voice of Jesus triumphantly declares that He has overcome death forever. "For as in Adam all die, even so in Christ shall all be made alive" (I Corinthians 15:22). The body will be laid aside, but the spirit will return unto God who gave it, there to await the resurrection of the body.

"I am the resurrection, and the life," Jesus said to Mary and Martha at the grave of Lazarus. "He that believeth in me, though he were dead, yet shall he live. And whosoever liveth and believeth in me shall never die. Believest thou this" (John 11:25-26). This is the voice of the Victor!

What do you believe about God? "Whom do men say that I am?" Jesus asked. Who do you say that He is?

Death may crush lives and break hearts; it may seem the apparent victor, but it shall not eternally triumph. One day God will take death's sting away, open the graves and reunite loved ones, abolishing death forever. "O death, where is thy sting? O grave, where is thy victory?" (I Corinthians 15:55). This is the voice of the Victor!

"The Lord himself shall descend from heaven with a shout," the apostle Paul wrote, "and with the trump of God; and the dead in Christ shall rise first" (I Thessalonians 4:16). This is the voice of the Victor!

Is your heart asleep to the things of Christ, or is He real to you today? God would say to you, "This is Jesus, My beloved Son. Hear Him!"

When we listen to Jesus, what do we hear? This blessed invitation: "Behold, I stand at the door and knock; if any man hear my voice, and open the door, I will come in to him, and will sup with him, and he with me" (Revelation 3:20). This is the voice of the Victor!

10

For there is one God, and one
mediator between God and man,
the man Christ Jesus

(I Timothy 2:5).

THE CONTINUING CHRIST

What is Christ doing now?

We have considered many things concerning the person and work of Jesus Christ, reviewing especially His death, resurrection, and ascension. But I am not sure that we have given sufficient thought to the *continuing* Christ.

Someone has said that to understand the gospel, you must understand the Book of Romans, and to understand both the law and the gospel, you must understand the Book of Romans and the Book of Hebrews. The key word throughout Hebrews is *better*: the better priest, the better prophet, the better covenant. Everything that the writer of Hebrews sets forth masterfully compares the law and the gospel, emphasizing the better things of grace as we find them in Jesus Christ. He is prophet, priest, and king. ". . . He ever liveth to make intercession for them [His own]" (Hebrews 7:25).

The earthly work of Jesus, from His birth, through His ministry to His death, resurrection, and ascension, is described plainly and in detail in the Gospels. But forty days after His resurrection, Jesus Christ ascended into heaven. He was received out of His disciples' sight. The angels told them, ". . . This same Jesus . . . shall so come in like manner . . ." (Acts 1:11).

But what is happening in heaven? We know that it is a per-fect paradise we cannot even imagine. But what is Jesus doing there now? What is the relation of Jesus Christ to His children today? The Bible says that all who are Christians are joint heirs with Christ. From the time of His ascension into heaven until He shall come back as victorious conqueror to earth, He is our Redeemer and Intercessor. He went beyond the curtain that separates heaven and earth into the divine Holy of Holies.

It is rather paradoxical that we have to say Jesus com-pleted His work — but yet it is being continued. The word "finished" can never be written over the work of Jesus. The Hebrew word that He uttered on the cross is three words in the English language: "It is finished" (John 19:30). In the Greek text it is only one word, which does not mean "finished" in the sense that it left nothing more to be added, but that it was ful-filled — the crucial event prophesied had come to pass. Even now, Christ is seeing to all that is necessary for the complete maturing of our salvation.

We recognize that His redemptive work of sacrifice for sin was completed on Calvary. Everything necessary for our salva-tion was done. It was finished in every sense that men know completion. But Jesus had about His work a perspective that none of us can know or understand. Seldom do we do any-thing but that a chance to do it over would be welcome, so that we might do it more perfectly. Whatever song you might sing, whatever message you might bring, whatever lesson you might teach, whatever responsibility you might fulfill — there so often comes the gnawing sense of incompleteness. If only we had that hour, that moment, to live over again! But Jesus ac-complished His purpose completely; nothing needed to be per-fected. "It is finished," He said. His sacrificial death shattered all the foes of God and opened the gates of redemption. It was the perfected work that Jesus had come to do.

It is a great thought today that He is the *remaining* Christ We have many things that remain. Our Bible remains. He said, "Heaven and earth shall pass away, but my words shall not pass away" (Matthew 24:35). Jesus Christ is *the same* yesterday, and today, and forever. The fact that He is the continuing Christ is one of the great miracles of all ages.

Jesus Christ is now in the presence of God. What then is His relationship to us there, and what does it have to do with our lives here? First of all, we would recognize that we have in Him an advocate, a friend at court.

The Proximity of God

Many Old Testament characters seemed to have longed for more closeness to God. Job expressed the desperate need that all men feel: "Oh, that I knew where I might find him [God] . . ." (Job 23:3). Job wanted to be able to pour out the emptiness of his soul, the sin of his life, the love of his heart. He longed to have a closer walk with God. If only God could be as real and near to him as He was to Adam and Eve! At first, God had fellowship with the pair He created in the Garden of Eden at the end of the day. Then, because of sin, the face of God was veiled from men. Job was not the first man — nor the last — to feel and express his need for God. All of us have great need for God in our lives.

Certainly God did not have to come to earth to understand the hearts of men. But it was necessary for Jesus to come to the earth that men might understand the heart of God. His coming brought God nearer to us. We came to know God as He was revealed in the person and face of Jesus Christ.

"I go to prepare a place for you," Jesus told His disciples (John 14:2). "But the Comforter, . . . the Holy Spirit, . . . the Father will send in my name, [and] he shall teach you all things . . ." (John 14:26). He is the Third Person of the Trinity, who continues the work of Jesus on earth. The Holy Spirit ". . . shall not speak of himself, but . . . He shall glorify me . . ." (John 16:13-14). He always praises Jesus. Those who give so much emphasis to the idea of the Holy Spirit need to recognize that nowhere in the Scriptures does He put Himself forward, but rather magnifies the Godhead of which He is a part. He brings God closer to us.

Jesus left this sin-cursed earth to go back to heaven, the Bible says, to sit down at the right hand of God. This indicates the nearness of Christ to His Father's heart. "The Lord said unto my Lord," wrote David, "Sit thou at my right hand, until I make thine enemies thy footstool" (Psalm 110:1; Mark 12:36). Part of the redemptive work of Jesus is to sit down beside the Father, having completed the sacrifice for our sins.

Priesthood of Christ

When Stephen was being stoned to death, the Bible says, "he, being full of the Holy Spirit, looking up steadfastly into heaven, and saw the glory of God, and Jesus standing on the right hand of God" (Acts 7:55). Jesus was not sitting, but *standing*. The only time in the Bible that we find God in a hurry is when He is pictured as the father running toward the prodigal son returning home (Luke 15:20). In the story of Stephen, we see the great interest on the part of Jesus when one of His children is dying. No longer is Jesus sitting, but standing!

Always He is looking this way. It is hard for us to comprehend God's mighty interest in us. God has been drawn close to us and we are drawn close to Him by the intercession of Jesus. That is why, when we pray to God, we pray in Jesus' name.

Talmage, a great preacher of the past who had a church in Brooklyn, once made some pastoral calls with his wife, leaving their child with a babysitter. When the parents, returning to the parsonage, opened the door, the child's back was toward them and he was playing quietly. But as soon as he saw his mother, he began to cry.

"What's wrong?" the mother asked.

"I hurt my hand."

"Why, I didn't see you hurt your hand," the mother said.

"I hurt my hand while you were away" the child insisted.

"Why didn't you cry then, instead of now?" the mother asked.

"Because I didn't have you to cry to," the child sobbed, running into his mother's arms.

There is a desolate feeling of loneliness in man, a frustration of longing that only God can satisfy. In Jesus we have one who understands us. The Bible says, "we have not an high priest who cannot be touched with the feeling of our infirmities" (Hebrews 4:15). Notice that it does not say He is touched *by* our infirmities, but He is touched *with* our infirmities — there is a vast difference!

Some take the attitude of those who passed by the injured man on the Jericho road. They looked down at him and were touched by the sight. "It is a terrible thing," they said sadly, shaking their heads, "Someone ought to do something!"

Even though we are touched by the sins of the lost world, we often withdraw, not wanting to get involved. Jesus didn't withdraw. He plunged into the very midst of human life. He involved Himself in our feelings and our infirmities. Our suffering is not a thing apart from Him; the suffering of His children is His own suffering, also.

Many years ago I went to stay at the home of a rancher one night after a meeting. "Preacher," he confided in me out of a heart full of sorrow, "if your children are not yet old enough to break your heart, you have never known what real heartbreak is!" He was suffering with, not apart from, his children; there is such a close bond between a child and his parents. In the same kind of relationship, Jesus would have us understand that He feels with us the same intensity of joy or pain — and to a much greater degree. "If ye then, being evil, know how to give good gifts unto your children," He said, "how much more shall your Father, who is in heaven, give good things to them that ask him?" (Luke 11:13).

He is touched *with* the feeling of our infirmities! We have a way of overlooking and minimizing the sufferings of others, but Jesus *knows* and understands the suffering of mankind. You and I can know and understand only partially. Others can understand your suffering only through comparison with whatever suffering they might have known. But not so with Jesus. There is no path to which we are called but that He has first gone before us to smooth the path and show us the way.

One day a mother brought a desperately sick child into a hospital and in the waiting room the child died. Neither the coaxing of the physician or anyone else could get the little mother to give up her baby. Her husband came from his work, but he could not persuade her.

A pastor was called, and finally, in the hospital corridor, he saw a woman who had lost a child. "You sit down by her and talk to her for a while," he suggested. That mother who had gone through the same bereavement sat down and poured out her heart of sympathy to the mother who was clutching her dead baby. After a few moments of sharing their sorrow, touched by the other woman's real understanding, the little mother reached out and put the lifeless body into her hands. But it was only after someone had sat down by her side and suffered *with* her.

God does not offer us a spectator religion. He is not sitting on the balcony of heaven unmindful of our burdens and problems in this life. In Christ, God is very real and very near. He understands the fine print of pain in our lives. He knows the silent heartaches, we cannot share with anyone. Jesus is "touched with the feeling of our infirmities." Nobody can say that Mohammed was touched with the sorrows of his people. The priests of false religions are not touched with the infirmities of their followers. But we can claim a great High Priest who suffers with us, who was tempted in all points that we are — yet without sin.

Promises of Strength

Therefore we find fulfilled in our lives the promises of Jesus. He said He would never leave us or forsake us.

He went back to heaven so that the Holy Spirit might come

to work for us and through us. There is suffering all over the world — not just in one country, one town, one home. To the Holy Spirit of God, there is no question of time or miles. We can come to our omnipresent High Priest in heaven with prayers that span time and distance, for through the Holy Spirit, Jesus can reach every heart.

Jesus is also the perfect priest. In the Old Testament, the priest was the man who mediated. He was a dedicated man who had to meet many special requirements for the priesthood. But even so, priests were only human and had many imperfections — just as the preachers in our pulpits today. But the priests performed a work of mediation; they offered the sacrifices, and then the High Priest took the blood into the Holy of Holies; he was the man who stood between God and men. But Jesus is called the Great High Priest (Hebrews 4:14). He is above all the others. Melchizedek, the ancient priest of the Old Testament, is pointed out as the pattern of the priesthood of Christ, who did not qualify by lineage as Aaron and others who were descended from Levi. The Bible does not mention the parentage of Melchizedek, or his death. The Aaronic priesthood descended from one generation to another. The Bible says Jesus is our High Priest who *ever liveth* to make intercession for us.

What is Jesus Christ doing now? He is removing the stumbling blocks between us and God. The Bible says that as we pray, He takes our thoughts and our utterances and deciphers their true meaning. He understands and makes them as they ought to be: "Here is what My child is saying," He says to the Father. He removes the obstacles of our ignorance and weakness. He remains there always to present our case at the throne of God.

The great priestly prayer of the Saviour is recorded in John 17. ". . . Those that thou gavest me I have kept," He said (v. 12). He is always keeping us.

He is always speaking about us, always concerned about us.

"I have prayed for thee," He said to Peter, "that thy faith fail not" (Luke 22:32). He is our praying priest.

He is our personal priest. Each of us has the right to come to the throne of God through Him. We can lay hold on the Father and say, "We have a Saviour and High Priest!" We have access to the throne of God, not because of anything good about us, but because of Him, our substitute.

Thus He is the perfect advocate. He is not only the sacrificial Lamb, without spot or blemish, He is not only the Lifegiver through His shed blood, but He is the Mediator between God and man.

When Jesus died that day on Golgotha's tree, God reached down from heaven and ripped the veil of the Temple from top to bottom. It would have taken the strength of about forty oxen to pull apart that heavily-woven linen curtain. Indeed, only the unseen hands of God could have reached to the top and rent it from top to bottom. No longer was God's Mercy Seat to be hidden; the way into His presence was opened for all eternity.

"Thou therefore, my son, be strong in the grace that is in Christ Jesus," Paul encouraged his protégé, Timothy (I Timothy 2:1). If you know Christ, then heaven is open to you. The ear of God, the presence of God, and the promises of God are available to you. We have, therefore, a *continuing* Christ, the Holy Son of God at the right hand of the Father, who ever lives to make intercession for us.

This